Serverless Ha

Swizec Teller | 2021

TABLE OF CONTENTS

TABLE OF CONTENTS

TABLE OF CONTENTS

TABLE OF CONTENTS

TABLE OF CONTENTS

TABLE OF CONTENTS

TABLE OF CONTENTS

TABLE OF CONTENTS

Getting Started with Serverless

Hello friend 🩶

I'm happy you're giving serverless a try. It's one of the most exciting shifts in web development since React introduced us to components.

Creating your first serverless application can be intimidating. Type "serverless" into Google and you're hit with millions of results all assuming you know what you're doing.

There's Serverless, the open source framework, then there's AWS Serverless, and a "serverless computing" Wikipedia article, your friends mention lambda functions, then there's cloud functions from Netlify and Vercel ... and aren't Heroku, Microsoft Azure, and DigitalOcean droplets a type of serverless too? *"CloudFlare edge workers!"* someone shouts in the background.

It's all one big mess.

That's why I created the Serverless Handbook. The resource I wish I had :)

Let's start with a short history lesson to get a better understanding of what serverless is and what it isn't. Then you'll build your first serverless backend – an app that says Hello 🌸

Don't want the intro? Jump straight to your first app at the end of this chapter.

What is serverless

> Serverless is other people's servers running your code.

The logical next step to platform as a service, which came from The Cloud, which came from virtual private servers, which came from colocation, which came from a computer on your desk running a web server. 🐱

First we all had servers.

You installed Linux on a computer, hooked it up to the internet, begged your internet provider for a static IP address, and let it run 24/7. Mine lived in the bedroom and I'll never forget that IP. Good ol' 193.77.212.100.

Figure 0.1: The world's first web server, a NeXT Computer

With a static IP address, you can tell DNS[1] servers how to find your server with a domain. People can type that domain into a URL and find your server.

But a domain doesn't give you a website or a webapp.

For that, you need to configure Apache or Nginx, set up a reverse proxy to talk to your application, run your application, ensure that it's running and ... it gets out of hand fast. Just to put up a simple website.

1 https://en.wikipedia.org/wiki/Domain_Name_System

Figure 0.2: A colocation server rack

Then came colocation

Colocation was a solution for the bedroom problem. What happens if your house catches fire? What if power goes out? Or Mom trips on the power cable and unplugs your computer?

Residential hosting is not reliable.

Your internet is lower tier than a business would get. Less reliable and if the provider needs to do maintenance, they think nothing of shutting off your pipes during non-peak hours. Your server needs strong internet 24/7.

When you go on vacation, nobody's there to care for your server. Site might go down for a week before you notice. 💀

Colocation lets you take that same server and put it in a data center. They supply the rack space, stable power, good internet, and physical security.

You're left to deal with configuration, maintenance, and replacing hard drives when they fail.

PS: Computers break all the time. A large data center replaces a hard drive every few minutes just because a typical drive lasts 4 years and when you have thousands, the stats are not in your favor.

It's on you to keep everything running.

Then came virtualization

Colocation solved physical problems, but not the fact that your servers are bored.

A typical server runs at about 30% utilization, which means you're wasting money.

Reasons for low utilization vary.

You have to keep the hardware happy and thermally content, you have to over-provision in case of traffic spikes or developer mistakes. Sometimes your site just isn't as popular as you'd like.

What if we could run multiple servers on the same machine?

The first type of virtualization were basic virtual hosts[2] . They let you run multiple websites on the same machine. A domain maps to an application on your computer, web server knows the mapping, and voila: sites can share resources.

Worked great but caused problems.

Websites on the same computer are *very* close together. You could hack one site and gain access to another. You could starve every website for resources by attacking 1 site with a lot of traffic. You could config yourself into a corner with overlapping configuration.

Virtual private servers[3] and later containerization[4] were the solution to that problem. Rather than multiple websites on the same machine, you can host *multiple whole computers* on the same machine. Like a computer with many brains. 🧠 .

The VPS – virtual private server – was born. Providers of "ssh access" became popular in the early 2000's. Pay a few bucks a month and you get a real live server on the internet. No hardware required.

You're on the hook for software setup and you share the machine with other users.

What if your site gets popular?

2 https://en.wikipedia.org/wiki/Virtual_hosting
3 https://en.wikipedia.org/wiki/Virtual_private_server
4 https://en.wikipedia.org/wiki/OS-level_virtualisation

The cloud is born

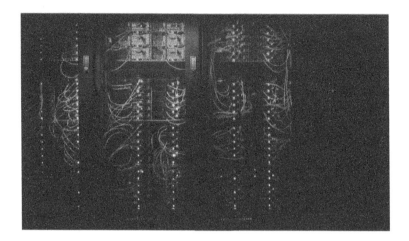

Early VPS was a lot like The Cloud. Computers running on the internet without touching hardware.

Where VPS struggled was scale.

Once your traffic started to grow, you'd need more servers to handle the load. There's only so much a single server can do every second.

And while computers are getting stronger and stronger (known as vertical scaling[5]), it's cheaper to share the load between a lot of small computers (horizontal scaling[6]).

But how do you ensure your servers are all the same? How do you spin them up quickly when traffic spikes on Black Friday?

5 https://en.wikipedia.org/wiki/Scalability#VERTICAL-SCALING
6 https://en.wikipedia.org/wiki/Scalability#VERTICAL-SCALING

You deal with it by hand.

Set up a server, make sure it works. Create a new server. Copy configuration. Create scripts for common tasks and spend hours making sure everything's okay.

Repeat for each new server. 💀

Cloud solves this problem with automation and containers. Docker[7] for containerization, kubernetes[8] for orchestration.

You start every new server from an image in your cloud provider's library. Comes with basic setup and common defaults. You add tweaks and create a new image.

The cloud provider gives you easy controls to create as many instances of that server as you'd like. Press a button, get a server.

Sometimes you can make it scale automatically. Scripts notice traffic rising and create new servers. When traffic subsides, the same scripts tear the servers back down.

7 https://en.wikipedia.org/wiki/Docker_(software)
8 https://en.wikipedia.org/wiki/Kubernetes

Platform as a Service

A variation on The Cloud is the PaaS[9] – platform as a service.

With PaaS you pay somebody else to deal with the cloud while you focus on code. They configure your servers and dockers and kubernetes and make everything play together. You build the app.

`git` push to deploy and voila. 👌

Many PaaS providers let you drop down a few levels and break everything. You get to mess with low level configs, operating system libraries, web servers, databases, etc. Empowering *and* dangerous. I tend to get it wrong.

While PaaS takes care of your servers, *you* have to take care of the "frontend". Set up domains and DNS, make your application run right for the platform, configure your own CDN[10], deal with static files, and so on.

The platform does servers.

9 https://en.wikipedia.org/wiki/Platform_as_a_service
10 https://en.wikipedia.org/wiki/Content_delivery_network

Serverless is born

Serverless[11] is the logical next step after PaaS.

Once you have a system that uses containers to automatically scale and descale based on demand, use repeatable configuration, and painless deploys … that's serverless right there.

Serverless's main innovation are *tiny* containers and the ecosystem of services and tools around it.

Server containers so tiny you can spin them up and down in milliseconds. They achieve this because the code they run is:

1. Small
2. Standardized
3. Does 1 thing

A serverless "server" is a function responding to an API endpoint. Request comes in, server wakes up, runs for a few milliseconds, and goes back to bed.

The platform takes care of optimization, configuration, and everything else. You get an input and return an output.

Servers never idle because they live as long as the request they're serving.

Biggest benefit of this approach?

11 https://en.wikipedia.org/wiki/Serverless_computing

Metered pricing. No more money wasted on idling servers waiting for requests. Pay for the time you're getting work done.

Your first serverless backend

In the next few minutes you're going to build your first serverless backend. A service that says Hello 👋

We're using open source technologies and deploying on AWS Lambda. You can learn about other providers in the Serverless Flavors[12] chapter.

12 https://serverlesshandbook.dev/serverless-flavors

You'll need a computer configured for JavaScript development: Have nodejs installed, a code editor, and a terminal.

Setup for serverless work

When working with serverless I like to use the open source Serverless[13] framework. We'll talk more about why in the Good serverless dev experience[14] chapter.

With the serverless framework we're going to configure servers using YAML files. You write config, framework figures out the rest.

Install it globally:

```
npm install -g serverless
```

You'll need AWS credentials too.

I recommend following Serverless's guide on AWS setup[15] . It walks you through the necessary steps on your Amazon account and a couple terminal commands to run.

13 https://github.com/serverless/serverless
14 https://serverlesshandbook.dev/serverless-dx
15 https://serverless.com/framework/docs/providers/aws/guide/credentials/

Create a tiny project

There are no special initializers for serverless projects. You start with a directory and add a configuration file.

```
mkdir hello-world
cd hello-world
touch serverless.yml
touch handler.js
```

You now have a project with 2 files:

- `serverless.yml` for configuration
- `handler.js` for server code

In future chapters you'll write backends using TypeScript. But one thing at a time :)

Configure your first server

Configuration for your server goes in `serverless.yml`. We're telling the Serverless framework that we want to use AWS, run nodejs, and that this is a dev project.

Then we'll tell it where to find the code.

```
# serverless.yml

service: hello-world

provider:
  name: aws
  runtime: nodejs12.x
  stage: dev
```

Our service is called `hello-world` and there's a couple details about our provider. The `stage` tells the difference between development, QA, and production deployments. More on that in the Dev, QA, and prod[16] chapter.

---

16 https://serverlesshandbook.dev/dev-qa-prod

Let's tell our server how to run code.

```yaml
# serverless.yml

service: hello-world

provider:
    name: aws
    runtime: nodejs10.x
    stage: dev

functions:
    hello:
        handler: ./handler.hello
        events:
            - http:
                path: hello
                method: GET
                cors: true
```

We started a functions section.

Each entry becomes its own tiny server – a serverless lambda. Together, they're the hello-world service.

The hello lambda calls an exported hello function inside our handler.js file when a GET request hits /hello.

All that from these few lines of code ✋

PS: enabling CORS[17] lets you call this function from other websites. Like your frontend app.

Write your first backend function

Backend functions in a serverless environment look like the JavaScript functions you're used to. Grab arguments, return a response.

Add a hello function to handler.js

```javascript
// handler.js

exports.hello = async (event) => {
  return {
    statusCode: 200,
    body: "Hello <span class='emoji'
     ↪  data-emoji='wave'> </span>",
  }
}
```

17 https://en.wikipedia.org/wiki/Cross-origin_resource_sharing

It's an async function that accepts a trigger event and returns a response. A success status with a Hello `<span class='emoji' data-emoji='wave'> </span>` body.

That's it. You wrote backend code. 🤘

Deploy your first serverless backend

To deploy, we run `serverless deploy`.

And your server is up.

You get a URL for your lambda and some debugging output. My URL is `https://z7pc0lqnw9.execute-api.\ us-east-1.amazonaws.com/dev/hello`, if you open it in your browser, it's going to say `Hello`

I'll keep it up because it's free unless somebody clicks. And when they do, current AWS pricing gives me 1,000,000 clicks per month for free 😅

Go to serverlesshandbook.dev/claim for interactive features.

What you got

The Serverless framework talked to AWS and configured many things.

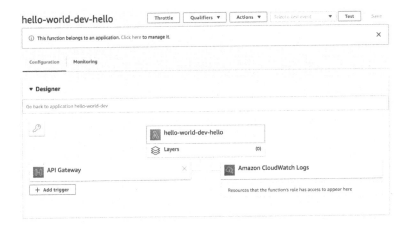

- **API Gateway** to proxy requests from the internet to your function
- **Lambda** to run your code. This is a tiny container that wakes up when called.
- **CloudWatch logs** to collect logs from your code. Helps with debugging.

All those are configured for you. No UI to click through, no config to forget about next time, nothing your friends have to set up to deploy the same code.

Exciting!

Next chapter, we talk about the pros & cons of using serverless in your next project.

Serverless Pros & Cons – when should you go serverless?

Okay you've heard of serverless, tried it out, and you think it's neat. But should you *really* go serverless for your next project?

Yes!

Most of the time ...

Serverless is a great option for most projects most of the time. You save configuration and maintenance time, gain flexibility, and in extreme cases spend more $$ per request than building your own servers.

Large apps can reach the cost curve limits of serverless. Bank of America, for example, announced $2B in savings[18] from building their own data centers.

You won't hit those issues. And if you do, I hope there's a business model to back it up and you can afford DevOps professionals. 😜

18 https://bit.ly/3swd5TR

Large orgs tend to provide a cloud or serverless-like environment internally. If you have access to that, use it.

Serverless is an ecosystem

When I say serverless, I don't mean just throwing up code on a function-as-a-service[19] platform like AWS Lambda. I'm talking about the whole ecosystem.

The core idea is this:

1. Backend does as little as possible
2. Clients tie everything together
3. Static files come from fast content delivery networks[20]
4. Database handles data consistency
5. As much work as possible happens at compile and deploy time

Users' and developers' machines do the hard work.

Is part of your app the same for every user? Package it up at deploy time. No need to bother the server *or* the client with that work.

Is part of your app specific to individual users? Let the client handle it. Every phone is a powerful computer these days.

19 https://en.wikipedia.org/wiki/Function_as_a_service
20 https://en.wikipedia.org/wiki/Content_delivery_network

Got dynamic data that needs to synchronize across multiple sessions or users? Background processes that aren't tied to a specific session? Perfect fit for your server and database.

We go in depth about this architecture in the chapter on Serverless Architecture Principles[21] .

Serverless pros

The main benefit of serverless is that you don't deal with servers. They're somebody else's problem.

You save time

You focus on *application* code. No more tedious maintenance tasks that aren't specific to your problem.

Bye bye yak shaving. 🐃

21 https://serverlesshandbook.dev/serverless-architecture-principles

"I need an API. That means I have to run a server. Which means I need Apache or Nginx to map HTTP requests to my app server. I need a computer to run all that. Which means I have to set up a whole operating system. Then I have to make sure everything runs at boot. And if a process goes down, it needs to restart. And ..."

After all that work you get to build your application.

With serverless **you save time otherwise spent managing servers.** Whether that's you personally or a DevOps team in your organization.

Programming productivity

You write backend code more productively.

Smaller, more self-contained code, ideally a single function, brings clarity and focus. Do one thing and do it well[22]

With increased focus, you get:

- easier testing
- quicker understanding
- shorter development cycles

22 https://en.wikipedia.org/wiki/Unix_philosophy#Do_One_Thing_and_Do_It_Well

Often cheaper

Serverless can be cheaper to run.

You save opportunity and employee cost *and* you're not paying for servers you aren't using.

As mentioned in the Getting Started[23] chapter: before serverless, you'd have to (over)provision a bunch of machines in case there's a traffic spike. That means you're paying for servers you aren't using.

With serverless, you pay per execution and run time. Like pay-as-you-go pricing: Run code, pay for that run.

When there's no traffic, there's no cost. 👍

Scalability

Google likes to call serverless architectures *from prototype to production to planet-scale.* You don't want to use serverless at planet scale though.

But Google is right: Serverless scales. A lot.

The details on *why* serverless is scalable are tricky to get into. It has to do with how much work you can pack into a single physical machine ... but there *is* a machine somewhere and you might run out of those with truly planet-scale work 💀

23 https://serverlesshandbook.dev/getting-started

It comes down to this: You're running a hyper-elastic server[24] that adapts to changes in workload at millisecond precision. In theory this gives you perfect utilization.

Serverless cons

As much as I think serverless is the next big thing in web development, it's not all fun and games out there. There *are* disadvantages to using serverless.

Higher latency for low workloads

Performance comes in two flavors:

1. Latency
2. Speed or bandwidth

Latency talks about how long it takes from making a request to getting a response. Speed talks about how long it takes to do work.

Each *execution* is fast because the code is small and servers are fast. A few milliseconds and you're done.

But *latency* can be high. You're hitting the server cold every time. That means each request waits for the computer to wake up.

24 https://en.wikipedia.org/wiki/Elasticity_(cloud_computing)

That's why providers keep servers live between requests. But only if requests come often enough.

For low traffic applications with low latency demands, you might need a constantly provisioned server.

Sometimes costly

As Bank of America found out[25] pay-as-you-go pricing gets expensive when used a lot.

Serverless providers charge based on number of requests and resources used. You pay for every request and every millisecond of computation. Known as "compute".

If you have a lot of requests or long runtimes, you can rack up the costs beyond what you'd pay with your own servers.

For example: You wouldn't want to train a machine learning model on a serverless architecture. Learned that painful lesson with my first startup in 2010 and GoogleAppEngine. Flicked the On switch and the credit card melted 🔥

Another bad case for serverless are high traffic applications. At millions of requests per second, you're better off on your own.

25 https://bit.ly/3swd5TR

Serverless becomes expensive at high loads. Where the balance tips depends on what you're doing, how much time you're saving, and how much it costs to do yourself.

Vendor lock-in

This one's simple: You're building on somebody else's infrastructure.

If that infrastructure changes, you're screwed. If they crank up the price, you're screwed. If you want to move, you're screwed. If you want to deploy your own, you're screwed.

You *can* do all those things, but it's a tedious and difficult task that might break your app. You're not building features or working on your business while you migrate.

Startups rarely live long enough to have this problem. Enterprises take defensive measures like multi-year contracts with strict service level agreements.

Avoid building architecture agnostic code. It's hard and you're not likely to need it.

Systems complexity

You're paying for the simplicity of your application code with system complexity. Individual functions are simpler and easier to test. Complexity comes from how they interact.

We'll talk more about that in the Robust Backend Design[26] chapter.

The verdict?

It depends. You will have to think about this yourself :)

Ping me on twitter[27], if you'd like some help.

I like to use a series of questions:

- "Will this require a lot of computation? if the answer is yes, I consider building my own servers.

26 https://serverlesshandbook.dev/robust-backend-design
27 https://twitter.com/swizec

- *"Will this have ridiculously high traffic?* if the answer is yes, I'd choose serverless because I hate doing DevOps. High traffic hopefully means I can afford a professional :)
- *"Is this a small side project idea?"* serverless all the way
- *"Does every request need to be served under 10ms?"* you're gonna have to roll your own

Next chapter, we're going to talk about different serverless providers.

AWS, Azure, Vercel, Netlify, or Firebase?

You've read the getting started[28] of serverless, you know the pros and cons[29] , and decided to use serverless in your next project.

Now what?

There's a bunch of providers with different features, different pricing, different developer experience, different focus ... how do you choose?

Having tried many of those providers myself (AWS, Netlify, Vercel, Firebase), here's how I think about it 👇

AWS

[30]

28 https://serverlesshandbook.dev/getting-started
29 https://serverlesshandbook.dev/serverless-pros-cons
30   /tmp/book-320/book-320/print-ready.pdf-14719/2_chapters/aws.amazon.com

AWS is the serverless workhorse. They offer everything from function-as-a-service to hosted blockchain and machine learning products.

Many other hosting providers use AWS. Heroku runs their dynos on EC2 instances, Netlify and Vercel use S3 for static files, Lambda for cloud functions, etc. The exact details are a secret, but we can guess.

Did you know AWS was more than half of Amazon's revenue[31] in 2019? It's a beast.

With over 165 services, it's impossible to try or even know all of AWS. A few that I've used are:

- **EC2** – old school cloud. You get a virtual computer, set it up, and you're in control. Runs forever unless you make it stop.
- **S3** – the standard solution for static files. Upload a file, get a URL, file stays there forever. Used for image and video assets, but can't run server code or host a website.
- **CloudFront** – a CDN[32] that integrates with S3. Point to static files via CloudFront and they go to a server nearest to your users. Works like a read-through cache, makes your apps faster.
- **IAM** – identity and account management. AWS forces you to use this to manage permissions. It's secure, tedious to set up, and a thorn in your butt. Until it saves your butt.

31 https://bit.ly/3m0sU2x
32 https://en.wikipedia.org/wiki/Content_delivery_network

- **AWS Secrets Manager** – a secure way to use secrets in your serverless apps. Not in code, not in environment variables, but a secure encrypted storage.
- **Lambda** – the poster child for serverless. One of the first to popularize function-as-a-service architectures. Write your function, Lambda handles the rest.
- **SQS** – simple queue service is a simple way to implement queues. It's best used for communication between services. Stores and retries messages if necessary.
- **SNS** – simple notification service. Similar to SQS but designed for broadcasting. Many listeners can read each message and every message is delivered just once.
- **DynamoDB** – a hosted JSON document storage. One of the quickest-to-setup ways to persist data in a serverless application. Save a JSON blob and read it later. Not recommended for relational data models.
- **RDS** – relational database service. Set up a Postgres or MySQL database and AWS handles the rest. Better fit for traditional data with lots of relations.
- **CloudWatch** – a logging system. Every service in AWS connects to CloudWatch to dump logs and other debug data. You can use it to trigger lambdas on a schedule.

AWS services add up fast. Every tool does *one* job. No tool does *your* job.

When to choose AWS

I use AWS when I want control over the developer experience and how the system fits together.

For example: I'd use AWS when my project involves data pipelines, coordinating between users, and complex backend logic. You know it's backend logic because it impacts multiple users on different devices.

When not to choose AWS

Where AWS becomes overkill are typical JAMstack apps. A static site with lots of frontend logic.

Hosting those on AWS is a pain whereas Netlify and Vercel make them a core feature.

Azure

Azure ... exists. Microsoft's answer to AWS and it's hard to find people in the wild who use it.

Popular in the enterprise world with companies that can't or won't use Amazon services. I would stay away unless there's a good reason.

33   /tmp/book-320/book-320/print-ready.pdf-14719/2_chapters/azure.microsoft.com

Firebase

Firebase is Google's answer to AWS. Kind of.

You can think of Firebase as a done-for-you backend for web and mobile apps. Set up an account, pick your options, and it's ready to go.

Right now there are 18 firebase services ranging from analytics to database and even machine learning. I've tried their database solution and it works great.

34   /tmp/book-320/book-320/print-ready.pdf-14719/2_chapters/firebase.google.com

This is less extensive than the AWS section and that's the point. Firebase doesn't want you to think about any of this.

When to choose Firebase

You get the backend in a box with Firebase. There's little setup.

You'll have to change how you write your frontend code so it hooks up with Firebase and ... that's about it.

Great for small demos and when you don't want to think about the backend at all.

When not to choose Firebase

Like with other Magic providers, you're in trouble as soon as you step off the beaten path. Or when you have a special requirement they didn't predict.

When that happens your choice is to either change your app or rebuild from scratch.

Netlify

35

Netlify is wonderful.   They invented everyone's favorite
JAMstack[36] buzzword.

Starting as a static site host for JavaScript-heavy applications,
Netlify now offers cloud functions, authentication, and other
backend functionality. Meant for simple backend tasks.

Among Netlify's biggest draws are:

35   /tmp/book-320/book-320/print-ready.pdf-14719/2_chapters/www.
netlify.com
36 https://en.wikipedia.org/wiki/Netlify#JAMstack

- a great web UI to manage your projects
- git integration for automated deploys
- custom URLs for every branch
- automatic CDN and SSL setup for your site
- app builds run on their servers
- you can run their infrastructure locally
- PR deploy previews
- great support for teams

When to choose Netlify

Netlify is one of the best funded startups in this arena. That can be an important factor.

They've been around long enough to rely on and are young enough that you'll get decent support, if you have issues. I find that to be a great balance :)

If you like a git- and UI- first mentality, Netlify is great.

When not to choose Netlify

Netlify is almost always a great choice for your web app. Their cloud function support can be cumbersome and malnourished. It doesn't feel like a focus.

If you like interacting with your sites via the command line, I've found Netlify to be less great.

Vercel

```bash
● ◉ ●                          bash

▲ my-site/ now
> Deploying ~/ACME/my-site under acme
> Using project my-site
> https://my-site-7q03y4pi5.now.sh/ [v2]
> Ready! Deployment complete
- https://my-site.acme.now.sh [in clipboard]
▲ my-site/ ▊
```

Vercel is wonderful. Netlify's direct competitor created by Silicon Valley veterans.

Vercel's focus, however, is different than Netlify's.

Where Netlify makes static deploys painless to configure and deploy via git and their UI, Vercel tries to make *any* app painless to deploy via their CLI. Command-line first, git and UI second.

Vercel's cloud function support is similar to Netlify's. Meant for small functionality and help with frontend tasks.

Among Vercel's biggest draws are:

- superb command line interface

37 /tmp/book-320/book-320/print-ready.pdf-14719/2_chapters/vercel.com

- configure-less deploys
- git integration for automated deploys
- custom URLs for every deploy
- automatic CDN and SSL setup for your site
- PR deploy previews
- app builds run on their servers
- great support for teams

When to choose Vercel

Vercel is almost always a great choice for your web app.

Honestly it's a toss up between Netlify and Vercel right now. They're both playing catch up. When one releases a new feature, the other gets it a few months later.

I like Vercel's command line interface and the fact I can run `vercel` in any project and it shows up on the internet. No clicking or config needed.

When not to choose Vercel

Vercel is best for frontend-heavy apps and when you're using their NextJS framework. Like Netlify, it feels unlikely their backend support will reach the full power of AWS.

Any project that fits on Netlify, fits on Vercel. Then it becomes a matter of preference and familiarity. Personally, I like Vercel's aesthetic and CLI focus. If you prefer clicking in a UI, go with Netlify.

So ... what to choose?

My preference is to put the frontend on Netlify or Vercel and the backend on AWS.

This gives me a balance between control, simplicity, and developer experience. We look at that in the next chapter.

Create a good serverless developer experience

What makes a good developer experience?

I asked Twitter and it was all over the place. A theme emerged:

> Good developer experience is when tools make
> your job easier, get out of the way, and let you
> focus on *your* code

How do you setup a serverless project for good DX?

It comes down to 3 features:

1. Infrastructure-as-code
2. Fast deploys
3. Tooling for common tasks

Infrastructure-as-code

stonks go skkrrrrrr
@muditameta

Replying to @Swizec

A setup that lets the developer work at their pace on building something without ever having to worry about tooling, CI, and other accidental complexity.
In other words, a setup optimized for iteration and low accidental complexity introduced noise.

7:21 PM · Nov 16, 2019

♡   ♡   🔗 Copy link to Tweet

As mentioned in the Getting Started[38] chapter, I like to use the open source Serverless Framework[39] with AWS. When using Netlify and Vercel you don't need Serverless because config-as-code is baked into their philosophies.

You write a configuration file, add it to version control, and that's your infrastructure. *Nothing* happens outside that configuration file.

This means that:

1. **Your deploys are repeatable**. Run deploy, get the same result every time. The same functions, the same queues, the same caching servers, everything.

---

38 https://serverlesshandbook.dev/getting-started#setup-for-serverless-work
39 https://en.wikipedia.org/wiki/Serverless_Framework

2. **Same infrastructure in test as in prod** Subtle differences between test environments and production are a waste of time. Big part of why Docker got popular.

3. **Share infrastructure between the team.** Ever had to ask a team member what environment variable they used for a thing? I have. After 2 hours of digging into the problem and realizing it's a configuration issue. 🙎

4. **Infrastructure that always fits your feature branch** A common problem are new features with different infrastructure. Like adding a new queue or cloud function. Instead of setting it up every time you test, infra-as-code can do it for you.

5. **Spend time in the tools you like, not confusing web UI** We're engineers and we like building things. Not clicking around a web UI doing repetitive tasks that take 20 minutes.

Fast deploys

> **Mikey**
> @CodingDive
>
> Replying to @Swizec
> An intuitive api and very short feedback cycles.
>
> 6:52 PM · Nov 16, 2019
>
> ♡ 1   ♢   🔗 Copy link to Tweet

The shorter your feedback cycle, the faster you can work.

On the frontend we have local dev servers and hot reloading. You see the result almost as fast as you write the code.

On the backend things are trickier.

You make a change ... now what? If you have unit tests, they show you part of the picture. The specific scenarios you thought to test, the methods you're exercising, the particular inputs.

All great.

But unit tests can't tell you your *system* works. That's where bugs come from – systems complexity.

You can simulate the environment and run your tests. That works to an extent, but it's never perfect.

Your best bet is to make deploying to a staging, QA, or production environment fast enough to use for development. With serverless, that becomes possible.

You could even set it up so that pushing to GitHub deploys every branch. Netlify and Vercel call it pull request previews.

How fast deploys work

Here's how the flow works:

0. Hit deploy
1. **Compile your code locally** on your fast developer machine. Since your code is small, it compiles in seconds.
2. **Compile your infrastructure** the serverless framework compiles your infrastructure into a config file for the target platform. With AWS that's SAM[40] .
3. **Upload your bundle** this is the slowest part.
4. **Infrastructure sets itself up** using your config the platform sets itself up. Servers appear, queues go up, etc. Takes a few seconds
5. **You're ready to go**

Slowest deploys I've seen on production-sized backends are in the 2 minute range. That's for a system with hundreds of lines of configuration.

40 https://aws.amazon.com/serverless/sam/

On my side projects it's 30 seconds.

That's fantastic compared to a Heroku or Docker deploy that takes 20 minutes.

Tooling for common tasks

I like to use my project's package.json as a collection of scripts for common tasks. yarn or npm run make them easy to run.

The most common is yarn deploy

```
# package.json

"scripts": {
    "build": "tsc build",
    "deploy": "npm run build && sls deploy"
}
```

With those 2 lines you can deploy from any branch without worry that you'll forget to build your project first. The build script runs a typescript build and sls deploy runs a serverless deploy.

This part gets trickier when you use multiple environments. We'll talk about that in the chapter on prod, QA, and staging environments[41].

Other helpful tools I've set up for bigger projects include:

- `yarn psql` to connect to my remote database
- `reset-env` to reset a remote database for testing
- `test-X` to run different tests against the server environment
- `add-engineer` to add a new engineer-specific environment so everyone can test on their own

Any time you find yourself running the same sequence of commands, you should consider adding them as a script to `package.json`. Give others that same super power :)

41 https://serverlesshandbook.dev/dev-qa-prod

How this works in practice

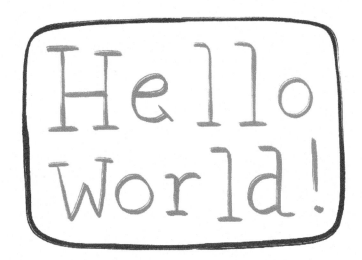

In the next few minutes you're going to build your first serverless backend. A service that says Hello 👋

We're using open source technologies and deploying on AWS Lambda. You can learn about other providers in the Serverless Flavors[42] chapter.

You'll need a computer configured for JavaScript development: Have nodejs installed, a code editor, and a terminal.

42 https://serverlesshandbook.dev/serverless-flavors

Setup for serverless work

When working with serverless I like to use the open source Server-less[43] framework. We'll talk more about why in the Good serverless dev experience[44] chapter.

With the serverless framework we're going to configure servers using YAML files. You write config, framework figures out the rest.

Install it globally:

```
npm install -g serverless
```

You'll need AWS credentials too.

I recommend following Serverless's guide on AWS setup[45]. It walks you through the necessary steps on your Amazon account and a couple terminal commands to run.

Create a tiny project

There are no special initializers for serverless projects. You start with a directory and add a configuration file.

43 https://github.com/serverless/serverless
44 https://serverlesshandbook.dev/serverless-dx
45 https://serverless.com/framework/docs/providers/aws/guide/credentials/

```
mkdir hello-world
cd hello-world
touch serverless.yml
touch handler.js
```

You now have a project with 2 files:

- serverless.yml for configuration
- handler.js for server code

In future chapters you'll write backends using TypeScript. But one thing at a time :)

Configure your first server

Configuration for your server goes in `serverless.yml`. We're telling the Serverless framework that we want to use AWS, run nodejs, and that this is a dev project.

Then we'll tell it where to find the code.

```
# serverless.yml

service: hello-world

provider:
  name: aws
  runtime: nodejs12.x
  stage: dev
```

Our service is called `hello-world` and there's a couple details about our provider. The `stage` tells the difference between development, QA, and production deployments. More on that in the Dev, QA, and prod[46] chapter.

46 https://serverlesshandbook.dev/dev-qa-prod

Let's tell our server how to run code.

```yaml
# serverless.yml

service: hello-world

provider:
    name: aws
    runtime: nodejs10.x
    stage: dev

functions:
    hello:
        handler: ./handler.hello
        events:
            - http:
                path: hello
                method: GET
                cors: true
```

We started a functions section.

Each entry becomes its own tiny server – a serverless lambda. To-gether, they're the hello-world service.

The hello lambda calls an exported hello function inside our handler.js file when a GET request hits /hello.

All that from these few lines of code 👋

PS: enabling CORS[47] lets you call this function from other websites. Like your frontend app.

Write your first backend function

Backend functions in a serverless environment look like the JavaScript functions you're used to. Grab arguments, return a response.

Add a hello function to handler.js

```javascript
// handler.js

exports.hello = async (event) => {
  return {
    statusCode: 200,
    body: "Hello <span class='emoji'
    ↪  data-emoji='wave'> </span>",
  }
}
```

47 https://en.wikipedia.org/wiki/Cross-origin_resource_sharing

It's an async function that accepts a trigger event and returns a response. A success status with a `Hello <span class='emoji' data-emoji='wave'> </span>` body.

That's it. You wrote backend code. ✌

Deploy your first serverless backend

To deploy, we run `serverless deploy`.

And your server is up.

You get a URL for your lambda and some debugging output. My URL is `https://z7pc0lqnw9.execute-api.\ us-east-1.amazonaws.com/dev/hello`, if you open it in your browser, it's going to say `Hello`

I'll keep it up because it's free unless somebody clicks. And when they do, current AWS pricing gives me 1,000,000 clicks per month for free 😛

Go to serverlesshandbook.dev/claim for interactive features.

What you got

The Serverless framework talked to AWS and configured many things.

- **API Gateway** to proxy requests from the internet to your function
- **Lambda** to run your code. This is a tiny container that wakes up when called.
- **CloudWatch logs** to collect logs from your code. Helps with debugging.

All those are configured for you. No UI to click through, no config to forget about next time, nothing your friends have to set up to deploy the same code.

Hello 🖐

Exciting!

Next chapter, we talk about designing your serverless architecture.

Architecture principles

What do you do when 3% of requests fail?

That was my reality one painful day in September. Deploy new feature, pat yourself on the back, go to lunch. A big feature – done. Nothing can touch you. 💪

Ding.

A Slack message? Who's working through lunch this time ...

Ding. Ding.

Weird, that's a lot of messages for lunchtime ...

BZZZ

Everything is on fire. High API error rate ⬚ an
alarm SMS

Our system sent alarms to Slack. Serious alarms to SMS.

The *high API error rate* was the biggest alarm. A catch-all that triggered when you can't be sure the more specific alarms even work.

Back to my desk, my heart sank: 3% of all API requests were failing. Reasons unknown.

Every user action, every background process on the web, on iOS *and* on Android, every time you opened the site or accessed the app 👉 3% chance of failure. At our usual 10 requests per second, that's 18 errors every minute!

Wanna know the best part?

Nobody noticed. ✌️

I knew something was wrong because of that SMS. The system kept hobbling along. Slower, in pain, but getting the job done.

How can a system with 18 failures per minute keep working?

Everything fails

The design principle behind every backend architecture states:

1. Everything can and will fail
2. Your system should work anyway

3. Make failures easy to fix

In 2011 Netflix forced engineers to think about this with the Chaos Monkey[48] in 2011. They wanted to *"move from a development model that assumed no breakdowns to a model where breakdowns were considered to be inevitable"*.

The Chaos Monkey makes that happen by introducing random failures to production environments. Servers down, databases unresponsive, message queues failing.

Reality is going to be your chaos monkey. Plan for it. 😉

How statistics play against you

At scale, you're playing against statistics. A one in a million error rate, at 10 requests per second, means an error every day.

Not a big deal, but if that error happens in your payment flow and you double charge a user ... they'll care.

What do statistics mean for you and your architecture?

AWS Lambda[49] guarantees a 99.95% monthly uptime percentage. That's your base error rate.

48 https://en.wikipedia.org/wiki/Chaos_engineering
49 https://aws.amazon.com/lambda/sla/

Even if you write the most perfect code, you can't have a lower error rate than your platform.

What does *99.95% monthly uptime percentage* mean in practice?

"Monthly Uptime Percentage" for a given AWS region is calculated as the average of the Availability for all 5-minute intervals in a monthly billing cycle. Monthly Uptime Percentage measurements exclude downtime resulting directly or indirectly from any Lambda SLA Exclusion.

"Availability" is calculated for each 5-minute interval as the percentage of Requests processed by Lambda that do not fail with Errors and relate solely to the provisioned Lambda functions. If you did not make any Requests in a given 5-minute interval, that interval is assumed to be 100% available.

Let's run the numbers

There are 24*60/5 = 288 5-minute intervals in a day. An average of 99.95% means that some intervals have lower availability, some higher. None go higher than 100%.

The hidden message is that you're going to see bursts of failures. A bad 5-minute period in a sea of 100% green. Outliers pull the average down.

Let's assume an even error rate to simplify the math.

At 1 request per 5 minutes, you get 288 * 0.9995 = 287.86 successful requests. Round up to 288. All good.

But at 1 per minute, you're down to 1439 successful requests. An error per day.

It gets worse from there.

I once built a large system running at a 0.092% failure rate. Lower than the *error* rate of the platform because of the architecture.

Pretty good eh?

1069 errors per day.

PS: *failure rate means the system never manages to process a request, error rate means individual, possibly recoverable, errors along the way*

How to design a resilient architecture

Resilience[50] is key. Designing your system to withstand shocks and errors. To work as a whole when individual pieces fail.

Your goal is to:

- **isolate errors** when an error happens, confine it to the smallest area possible without damaging the rest of your system
- **make operations replayable** triggering the same operation multiple times must produce the same result
- **retry until success** errors are often transient and go away when you try again
- **make your system debuggable** store enough information about your actions so that you can look back later

50 https://en.wikipedia.org/wiki/Resilience_(engineering_and_construction)

- **remove unprocessable requests** sometimes requests can't be processed. Make sure these don't kill your system or get in the way of valid requests
- **alert the engineer when something is wrong** errors can be part of normal operations. When there's too many, make your system cry out in pain and tell you where it hurts

You can achieve all that with a few steps.

Small, isolated, replayable operations

Think of your task as a pipeline.

A request comes in. You do X, then you do Y, then Z, then the result comes out. The request is your input, the result is your output.

Like Henry Ford's famous assembly line ☞ steel comes in the factory on one end, cars leave on the other.

For max resilience, make each operation follow this algorithm:

- get request
- check if request already processed
- if processed, finish
- if not, do your thing
- trigger the next step
- mark request as processed

Every request needs an identifier. Easiest if it's a unique id of a database row.

Having a way to answer *"Did I process this yet?"* gives you replayability. Call the same action with the same request twice and nothing happens.

Easiest way to achieve this, is a lookup table. I like to put a processed flag in each database row. Lets you pass a reference to the row between actions. Each does its thing and changes the flag.

Each action does one thing and one thing only.

Because each action performs one step in the process, you can look at the processed flags to see what's up.

Debugging becomes easier. You can test steps in the process on their own. Like a function call.

Isolation comes from decoupling

Isolation ensures that an error in one action doesn't impact others. *That* action fails and the pipeline might get backed up, but other actions keep working fine.

And because you have replayability, you can retry until your action succeeds. ✌️

Retry until success

Fire an action, get success or fail. If success, remove message from the queue and move on. If it fails, put message back on queue and try again.

Errors can be temporary. Engineers will fix the bug.

If it's a hardware problem, you can wait until your function runs on a different physical machine. Yay serverless.

You can keep retrying until success because actions are safely re-playable.

To be safe, I like to have a **cleanup worker** that goes through the database every few hours and checks for rows that failed to process and stopped retrying.

Catches errors in the retry system itself. ✌️

PS: more on queues and how this works in the chapter on serverless elements[51]

A debuggable system is a good system

Small actions that store a *"Yes I Did It"* state for each piece of data are easier to debug. You can look at your database to see which step failed.

51 https://serverlesshandbook.dev/serverless-elements

Replayability lets you trigger the failed action for that data and see what happens.

Since actions are functions and your messages are plain data, you can test locally. Unit tests are great, running production code on production data in your terminal, that's wow.

And if that's not enough, add logging. A well-placed `console.log` can do wonders.

Conclusion

> Build your system out of small isolated pieces
> that talk to each other via queues.

Next chapter we dive into queues and lambdas, and talk about how to tie them together into a system.

Elements of serverless – lambdas, queues, gateways, etc

Serverless is about combining small elements into a whole. But what are the elements and how do they fit together?

We mentioned lambdas, queues, and a few other in previous chapters – Architecture Principles[52] and Serverless Flavors[53]. Let's see how they work.

Lambda – a cloud function

"Lambda" comes from lambda calculus[54] - a mathematical definition of functional programming that Alonzo Church introduced in the 1930s. It's an alternative to Turing's turing machines[55]. Both describe a system that can solve any solvable problem[56]. Turing machines use iterative step-by-step programming, lambda calculus uses functions-calling-functions functional programming.

Both are equal in power.

AWS named their cloud functions AWS Lambda. As the platform grew in popularity, the word "lambda" morphed into a generic term for cloud functions. The core building block of serverless computing.

52 https://serverlesshandbook.dev/serverless-architecture-principles
53 https://serverlesshandbook.dev/serverless-flavors
54 https://en.wikipedia.org/wiki/Lambda_calculus
55 https://en.wikipedia.org/wiki/Turing_machine
56 https://en.wikipedia.org/wiki/Church%E2%80%93Turing_thesis

A lambda is a function. In this context, a function running as its own tiny server triggered by an event.

Here's a lambda function that returns "Hello world" in response to an HTTP request.

```typescript
// src/handler.ts

import { APIGatewayEvent } from "aws-lambda";

export const handler = async (event: APIGatewayEvent) => {
    return {
        statusCode: 200
        body: "Hello world"
    }
}
```

The TypeScript file exports a function called handler. The function accepts an event and returns a response. The AWS Lambda platform handles the rest.

Because this is a user-facing API method, it accepts an AWS API Gateway event and returns an HTTP style response. Status code and body.

Other providers and services have different events and expect different responses. A lambda always follows this pattern ☞ **function with an event and a return value.**

Considerations with lambda functions

Your functions should follow functional programming principles:

- **idempotent** – multiple calls with the same inputs produce the same result
- **pure** – rely on the arguments you're given and nothing else. Your environment does not persist, data in local memory might vanish.
- **light on side-effects** – you need side-effects to make changes like writing to a database. Make sure those come in the form of calling other functions and services. *State inside your lambda does not persist*
- **do one thing and one thing only** – small functions focused on one task are easiest to understand and combine

Small functions work together to produce extraordinary results. Like this example of combining Twilio and AWS Lambda to answer the door[57] .

---

57 https://swizec.com/blog/how-i-answer-the-door-with-aws-lambda-and-twilio/
swizec/9255

Creating lambdas

In the open source Serverless Framework, you define lambda functions with `serverless.yml` like this:

```
functions:
    helloworld:
        handler: dist/helloworld.handler
        events:
            - http:
                path: helloworld
                method: GET
                cors: true
```

Define a `helloworld` function and say it maps to the `handler` method exported from `dist/helloworld`. We're using a build step for TypeScript - the code is in `src/`, we run it from `dist/`.

`events` lists the triggers that run this function. An HTTP GET request on the path `/helloworld` in our case.

Other typical triggers include Queues, S3 changes, CloudWatch events, and DynamoDB listeners. At least on AWS.

Queue

Queue is short for message queue[58] – a service built on top of queue, the data structure[59]. Software engineers aren't that inventive with names 🦋

You can think of the queue data structure as a list of items.

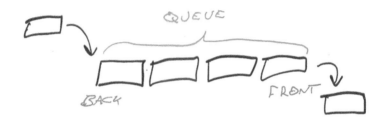

enqueing adds items to the back of a queue, dequeing takes them out the front. Items in the middle wait their turn. Like a lunch-time burrito queue. First come first serve, FIFO for short (first in first out).

A messaging queue takes this data structure and scales it into a service.

Different implementations exist and they all share these core properties:

- **persistent storage** – queues have to be reliable and store

58 https://en.wikipedia.org/wiki/Message_queue
59 https://en.wikipedia.org/wiki/Queue_(abstract_data_type)

messages in a database. Most queues prioritize speed and use in-memory storage like Redis.

- **a worker process** – once you have messages, you need to process them. A process periodically checks, if there's something new (polling)[60] . Another approach is to trigger this check every time a message arrives.
- **a trigger API** – when the queue sees a new message, it runs your code. In serverless that means running your lambda, in traditional environments it's another worker process.
- **a retry/error policy** – queues help you deal with errors. When you fail to process a message, it goes back on the queue and gets retried later.

Many modern queues add time to the mix. You can *schedule* messages for later. 2 seconds, 2 minutes, 2 days, ... Some queues limit how long messages can stick around.

Time helps with errors

Server processes can fail for any reason at any time[61] . For temporary errors a queue can use exponential backoff[62] when retrying. Giving your system more and more time to recover from issues.

Try to process a message. It fails. Try after 1 second. Fails. Retry in 2 seconds. Fail. 4 seconds ...

60 https://en.wikipedia.org/wiki/Polling_(computer_science)
61 https://serverlesshandbook.dev/architecture-principles
62 https://en.wikipedia.org/wiki/Exponential_backoff

I've seen corrupt messages, known as poison pills, backing off days into the future. We talk about handling unprocessable messages in the Robust Backend Design[63] chapter.

Defining a queue

AWS SimpleQueueService is a great queue service for the AWS serverless ecosystem. More powerful alternatives exist, but require more setup, more upkeep, and have features you might not need.

> Always use the simplest and smallest service that solves your problem until you know *why* you need more ✌

Using the serverless framework, you define an SQS queue in the resources section like this:

```
resources:
    Resources:
        MyQueue:
            Type: "AWS::SQS::Queue"
```

63 https://serverlesshandbook.dev/robust-backend-design

```
    Properties:
        QueueName: "MyQueue-${self:provider.stage}"
```

A resource named MyQueue of the SQS Queue type with a queue
name of MyQueue-{stage}. Adding the stage to your queue name
allows different logical environments without collisions. More on
that in the Dev, QA, and Prod chapter[64]

Make sure you use correct capitalization. The second Resources
must be capitalized, so do Type, Properties, and QueueName.

Capitalization matters because you're dropping a layer below
Serverless and writing AWS's native Serverless Application Model
(SAM) configuration. It's what your config compiles to before
deploying.

Processing a queue

You need a lambda to process messages on MyQueue.

```
functions:
    myQueueProcess:
```

---

[64] https://serverlesshandbook.dev/dev-qa-prod

```
handler: dist/lambdas/myQueue.handler
events:
    - sqs:
        arn:
            Fn::GetAtt:
                - MyQueue
                - Arn
        batchSize: 1
```

A lambda that runs each time MyQueue has a new message to process. With a batchSize of 1, each message runs its own lambda – a good practice for initial implementations. More about batch sizes in the Lambda Workflows[65] and Robust Backend Design[66] chapters.

The strange yaml syntax reads as: *an SQS event fired by a queue with the ARN identifier of getAttribute(Arn) from MyQueue.* Amazon Resource Names, ARN, are unique identifiers for each resource in your AWS account.

The myQueue.handler lambda would look like this:

65 https://serverlesshandbook.dev/lambda-workflows
66 https://serverlesshandbook.dev/robust-backend-design

```
import { SQSEvent, SQSRecord } from "aws-lambda";

export const handler = async (event: SQSEvent) => {
    // N depends on batchSize setting
    const messages: string[] = event.Records.map(
        (record: SQSRecord) => record.body
    );

    // do something with each message
    // throw Error() on fail

    return true;
};
```

An async function that accepts an SQSEvent, which contains multiple messages depending on batchSize. Never assume the total number because that setting might change.

Extract messages into an array of strings and process with a loop. Throw an error when something goes wrong so SQS can retry. Return true on success.

SNS

A useful alternative to SQS is the Simple Notification Service – SQS. Similar behavior, except you can't store messages on the queue.

With SNS each message sends *once*. If you don't catch it, it's gone.

But unlike SQS, each message can trigger multiple services.

API Gateway

You might not realize this, but servers don't talk directly to the internet.

WHAAAAAAAAAAAAAAAAT?

Application servers are protected by a reverse proxy[67] – a server that specializes in taking raw internet requests and routing them.

67 https://en.wikipedia.org/wiki/Reverse_proxy

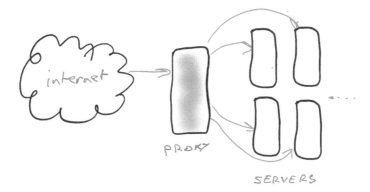

Requests come from the wild internet into the proxy. The proxy then decides:

- is this a valid request?
- will this request break the system?
- which type of server can handle this?
- which instance of that server should do it?

Validating requests can involve checking for denial of service attacks, verifying permissions, firewall protection, and even A/B testing.

Once verified the request goes to an instance of your application server. This is where horizontal scaling[68] comes into play.

Amazon calls their reverse proxy service API Gateway.

Other providers might have different names and they all perform the same function: Take request from the internet and pass it on to your lambda.

68 https://en.wikipedia.org/wiki/Scalability#HORIZONTAL-SCALING

Static file storage – S3

The serverless world is ephemeral which means you can't save files just anywhere.

Adding large files to your code makes starting new containers slow. You can't save locally because your server disappears after each request.

Static file storage services solve that problem.

AWS S3 is the most common. Other hosting services often act as an S3 abstraction. Pundits have called S3 the 8th wonder of the world.

Corey Quinn
@QuinnyPig

I know that @awscloud S3 is basically the eighth wonder of the world, but Athena is pretty damned close behind it.

Amazing, amazing product.

8:28 PM · Jan 24, 2020

♡ 487   ♡ 78   🔗 Copy link to Tweet

You can think of S3 as a hard drive with an API. Read and write files, get their URL, change permissions, etc.

Each file gets a URL that's backed by a server optimized for static files. No code, no dynamic changes. A raw file flying through HTTP.

Static file server – CDN

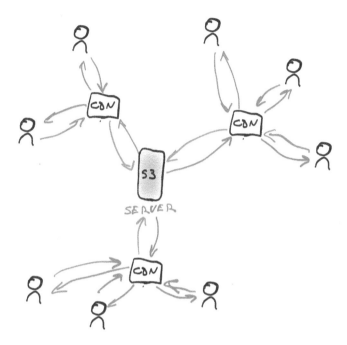

CDNs – content delivery networks[69] – are the next step in serving static file. They're like a distributed caching system.

Where S3 serves files from a central location, a CDN serves those same files from as close to the end user as possible. That speeds up your website by reducing latency.

Configuration on your end goes like this:

1. Point the CDN to your static file URL

69 https://en.wikipedia.org/wiki/Content_delivery_network

2. The CDN gives you a new URL
3. Use *that* URL in your client-side code

You can automate this part with build tools. Netlify and Vercel both handle it for you.

Now when a browser requests a file, the URL resolves to the nearest server. Request goes to that server and if the file is there, it's served. If there's no file, the CDN goes to your original source, caches the file, and *then* sends it back to the user.

And now your JavaScript, HTML, images, fonts, and CSS are fast to load anywhere in the world. 👌

Logging

Logging is one of the hardest problems in a distributed multi-service world. You can't print to the console or write to a local file because you can't see the console and files vanish after every request.

What do you do?

You use a logging service to send logs to a central location.

Implementing a logging service yourself is tricky (I've done it, do not recommend). The AWS ecosystem has you covered with CloudWatch.

CloudWatch UI tools lack filtering and graphing features you'd want as a power user, but it's a great start.

Anything you `console.log` is collected in CloudWatch alongside default logs.

Those are the important elements

Now you know the most important elements of your serverless ecosystem:

- lambdas for doing things
- queues for communicating
- gateways for handling requests
- S3 for static files
- CDN for serving static files
- logging to keep track

There's a bunch more to discover, but that's the core. Next chapter we look at using these to build a robust system.

Robust backend design

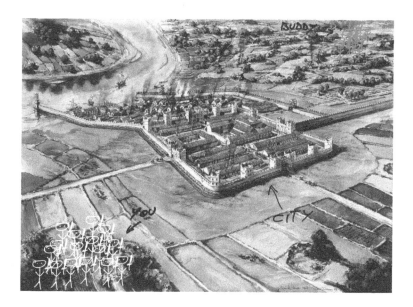

Figure 0.3: Two Generals Problem

Imagine you're a Roman general leading a vast and powerful army. You're about to attack a city.

But you can't do it alone.

Your buddy with another vast and powerful army hides behind a hill on the other side. You need their help to win.

Attack together and win. Attack alone and die.

How do you ensure a joint attack?

Smoke signals would reveal your plan to the city. It's too far to shout and phones are 2000 years in the future.

A messenger is your best bet. Run to the other army, deliver the message, come back with confirmation.

Unless they're caught. 👻

The messenger could fail to deliver your message. Or get caught on their way back. You'll never know.

Send more messengers until one makes it back? How does your friend know that any messenger made it back? Nobody wants to attack alone.

This puzzle is known as the Two Generals' Problem[70] . **There is no solution.**

No algorithm guarantees 100% certainty over a lossy medium. Best you can do is *"Pretty sure."*

And that's why distributed systems are hard.

You cannot have 100% reliability. As soon as servers talk to each other, you're doomed to probabilities.

Serverless systems are always distributed. 😵

70 https://en.wikipedia.org/wiki/Two_Generals%27_Problem

Build a robust backend

A robust backend keeps working in the face of failure.

As we mentioned in the Architecture Principles chapter[71] , your backend follows 3 principles:

1. Everything can and will fail
2. Your system should keep working
3. Failures should be easy to fix

You get there with a combination of error recovery, error isolation, and knowing when your system needs help.

The strategies mentioned in Architecture Principles[72] were:

- isolate errors
- retry until success
- make operations replayable
- be debuggable
- remove bad requests
- alert the engineer when something's wrong
- control your flow

This chapter talks about how.

71 https://serverlesshandbook.dev/serverless-architecture-principles
72 https://serverlesshandbook.dev/serverless-architecture-principles

Isolate errors

In March 2017, Amazon S3 went down[73] and took with it half the internet. Root cause was a typo.

AWS Engineers were testing what happens when a few servers go offline. A typo took out too many and the rest got overwhelmed. They started failing one by one.

Soon the whole system was down.

And because AWS relies on S3 to store files ... much of AWS went down. And because half the internet runs on AWS ... it went down.

AWS couldn't even update their status dashboard because error icons live on S3.

73   https://www.theverge.com/2017/3/2/14792442/amazon-s3-outage-cause-typo-internet-server

To isolate errors you have to reduce inter-dependency. Always think: *"What can I do to make moving pieces less dependent on each other?"*

In your car, the brakes keep working even if your brake lights go out. The systems work together, but independently.

Inter-dependency can be subtle and hard to spot. The specifics are different each time.

Here are 3 rules:

1. Give each operation a single responsibility
2. Do the whole operation in one atomic go
3. Avoid coupling

Serverless functions are optimized for this approach by default. They encourage you to keep code light and isolated 🐰

Give each operation a single responsibility

Think of serverless code like a function. How big are your functions? How much do they do?

Say you were building a basic math module. Would you write a function that performs plus *and* minus?

```
function doMath(a: number, b: number, op: string) {
    if (op === 'plus') {
        return a+b
    }else{
        return a-b
    }
}
```

That looks odd to me. Plus and minus are distinct operations.

You'd write 2 functions instead:

```
function plus(a: number, b: number) {
    return a + b
}

function minus(a: number, b: number) {
    return a - b
}
```

That's easier to work with.

Splitting your code into small operations is an art. Big functions are hard to debug and too many small functions are hard to understand.

My rule is that when I use "and" to describe a function, I need a new function.

Do the whole operation in one atomic go

Atomic operations guarantee correctness. Perform an action start to finish without distraction.

Say you're taking an important memory medicine.

You grab the pill bottle, take out a pill, put it on your desk, get an email and start reading. You elbow the pill off your desk.

10 minutes later you look down and there's no pill. Did you take it?

Same thing happens when your lambdas do too much. Your code can get distracted, halfway failures happen, and you're left with a corrupt state.

Recovering from corrupt state is hard.

Instead, try to avoid distractions. Keep operations small, go start to finish, delegate. Let another process read email. And clean up when there's an error[74] .

Avoid coupling

With atomic operations and delegating heavy work to other functions, you're primed for another mistake: Direct dependency.

Like this:

```
function myLambda() {
    // read from db
    // prep the thing

    await anotherLambda(data)
```

74 https://en.wikipedia.org/wiki/Atomicity_(database_systems)

```
    // save the stuff
}
```

You're coupling your myLambda function to your anotherLambda function. If anotherLambda fails, the whole process fails.

Try decoupling these with a queue. Turn it into a process. myLambda does a little, pushes to the queue, anotherLambda does the rest.

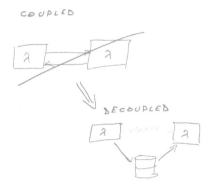

You can see this principle in action in the Lambda Pipelines for distributed data processing[75] chapter.

75 http://serverlesshandbook.dev/lambda-pipelines

Retry until success

Retrying requests is built into the serverless model.

AWS retries every lambda invocation[76], if the call fails. The number of retries depends on who's calling.

API Gateway is proxying requests from users and that makes retries harder than an SQS queue which has all the time in the world.

Retries happen for two reasons:

1. Lambda never got the message
2. Lambda failed to process the message

#1 is out of your control. Two generals problem struck between request and your code. 💩

#2 means you should always throw an error when something goes wrong. Do not pretend.

Both SQS – Simple Queue Service – and SNS – Simple Notification Service – support retries out of the box. They're the most common ways AWS services communicate.

Details on how each implements retries differ. You can read more about How SNS works[77] and How SQS works[78] in AWS docs.

76 https://docs.aws.amazon.com/lambda/latest/dg/invocation-retries.html
77 https://docs.aws.amazon.com/sns/latest/dg/sns-message-delivery-retries.html
78   https://docs.aws.amazon.com/AWSSimpleQueueService/latest/SQSDeveloperGuide/sqs-basic-architecture.html

Both follow this pattern:

1. Message accepted into SQS / SNS
2. Message stored in multiple locations
3. Message sent to your lambda
4. Wait for lambda to process or fail
5. If processed, remove message
6. If failed, retry ... sometimes thousands of times

Wait to delete the message until after confirmation. You might lose data otherwise.

Keep this in mind: never mark something as processed until you know for sure

Build replayable operations

Your code can retry for any reason. Make sure that's not a problem.

Follow this 4 step algorithm:

1. Verify work needs doing
2. Do the work
3. Mark work as done
4. Verify marking it done worked

Two Generals Problem may strike between you and your database 😵

In pseudocode, functions follow this pattern:

```
function processMessage(messageId) {
    let message = db.get(messageId)

    if (!message.processed) {
        try {
            doTheWork(message)
        } catch(error) {
            throw error
        }
        message.processed = true

        db.save(message)

        if (db.get(messageId).processed) {
            return success
        } else {
            throw "Processing failed"
        }
    }

    return success
}
```

This guards against all failure modes:

1. Processing retried, but wasn't needed
2. Work failed
3. Saving work failed

Make sure doTheWork throws an error, if it fails to save. Common cause of spooky dataloss. ✌

Be debuggable

Debugging distributed systems is hard. More art than science.

You'll need to know or learn your system inside-out. Tease it apart bit by bit.

Keeping your code re-runnable helps. Keeping your data stored helps. Having easy access to all this helps.

When debugging distributed systems I like to follow this approach:

1. Look at the data
2. Find which step of the process failed
3. Get the data that failed
4. Run the step that failed
5. Look at logs

You can use a debugger to step through your code locally. With a unit test using production data. But it's not the same as a full production environment.

If local debugging fails, add logs. Many logs. Run in production, see what happens.

*Being debuggable therefore means:

1. Safely replayable operations
2. Keep intermediate data long enough
3. Manually executable with specific requests
4. Identifiable and traceable requests (AWS adds requestId to every log)
5. Locally executable for unit testing

Remove bad requests

Requests can include a poison pill – a piece of bad data you can never process. They might swamp your system with infinite retries.

Say you want to process requests in sequence.

9 requests go great, the 10th is a poison pill. Your code gets stuck trying and retrying for days.

Meanwhile users 11 to 11,000 storm your email crying that the service is down. But it's not down, it's stuck.

Dead letter queues[79] can help. They hold bad messages until you have time to debug.

Each queue-facing Lambda gets two queues:

1. The trigger queue
2. A dead letter queue for bad requests

Like this in `serverless.yml`:

```
# serverless.yml

functions:
    worker:
        handler: dist/lambdas/worker.handler
        events:
                # triggering from SQS events
            - sqs:
```

79 https://en.wikipedia.org/wiki/Dead_letter_queue

```yaml
          arn:
            Fn::GetAtt:
              - WorkerQueue
              - Arn
          batchSize: 1

resources:
    Resources:
      WorkerQueue:
          Type: "AWS::SQS::Queue"
          Properties:
            QueueName:
↪ "WorkerQueue-${self:provider.stage}"
              # send to deadletter after 10 retries
              RedrivePolicy:
                deadLetterTargetArn:
                  Fn::GetAtt:
                    - WorkerDLQueue
                    - Arn
                maxReceiveCount: 10
      WorkerDLQueue:
          Type: "AWS::SQS::Queue"
          Properties:
            QueueName:
↪ "WorkerDLQueue-${self:provider.stage}"
              # keep messages for 14 days,
              # helps debug
              MessageRetentionPeriod: 1209600
```

A worker lambda runs from an SQS queue. When it fails, messages are retried.

Now all you need is an alarm on dead letter queue size to say *"Hey something's wrong, you should check"*.

Bug in your code? Fix the bug, re-run worker from dead letter queue. No messages are lost.

Bad messages? Drop 'em like it's hot.

Alert an engineer

The challenge with serverless systems is that you can't see what's going on. And you're not sitting there staring at logs.

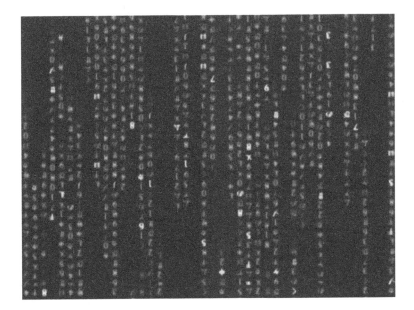

You need a monitoring system. A way to keep tabs on your services and send alerts. Email for small problems, slack for big problems, text message for critical problems.

That's what works for me.

AWS has basic monitoring built-in, Datadog is great for more control. More on monitoring in the Monitoring serverless apps chapter[80]

Control your flow

Control your flow means looking at the performance of your system as a whole.

Writing fast code is great, but if your speedy lambda feeds into a slow lambda, you're gonna have a bad day. Work piles up, systems stop, customers complain.

You want to ensure a smooth flow through the whole system.

Computer science talks about this through Queuing theory[81] and stochastic modeling[82] . Business folk talk about Theory of constraints[83] .

It's a huge field :)

80 https://serverlesshandbook.dev/serverless-monitoring
81 https://en.wikipedia.org/wiki/Queueing_theory
82 https://en.wikipedia.org/wiki/Stochastic_process
83 https://en.wikipedia.org/wiki/Theory_of_constraints

We talk more about flow in the Serverless performance[84] chapter.

Conclusion

In conclusion, a distributed system is never 100% reliable. You can make it better with small replayable operations, keeping code debuggable, and removing bad requests.

Next chapter we look at where to store your data.

84 https://serverlesshandbook.dev/serverless-performance

Databases and serverless

Serverless systems don't have a hard drive, where does your data go? You need a database.

But how do you choose which database and where do you put it? It depends.

Every database has advantages and disadvantages. Always fit your tech to your problem, not your problem to your tech.

First, what is a database? It's a system for storing and organizing data[85] .

> A database is an organized collection of data, generally stored and accessed electronically from a computer system.

Every database technology gives you these features:

- keeps your data
- lets you query data
- lets you update data

Keeping data is the difference between a cache[86] and a database. You can have an in-memory database for speed, but that doesn't make it a cache.

85 https://en.wikipedia.org/wiki/Database
86 https://en.wikipedia.org/wiki/Cache_(computing)

How to choose a database

Databases seek to find a balance between different optimization criteria. Your choice depends on how that balance fits the problem you're solving.

The common criteria are:

1. Speed of reading data
2. Speed of writing data
3. Speed of updating data
4. Speed of changing the shape of data
5. Correctness of data
6. Scalability

Notice how the list is about speed? That's because speed of data access is the biggest predictor of app performance.

I've seen API endpoints hit the database 30+ times. Queries that take 10ms instead of 1ms can mean the difference between a great user experience and a broken app.

ACID – a database correctness model

We'll focus on speed in this chapter. But to gain speed and scalability, databases sacrifice correctness. It's important that you know what correctness means in a database context.

Traditional databases follow the ACID model[87] of transactional correctness. A transaction being a logical operation on your data.

- **Atomicity** ensures that operations inside a transaction succeed or fail together and aren't visible until they all succeed
- **Consistency** ensures your data is in a valid state and doesn't become corrupted by a half-failed transaction
- **Isolation** ensures transactions executed in parallel behave the same as if they happened one after another
- **Durability** ensures that once a transaction succeeds, it stays succeeded and the data doesn't vanish

Certain databases add additional levels of logical correctness on top of the ACID model. We'll talk about those later.

Goals of the ACID model might remind you of the Architecture Principles[88] chapter. That's because it aims to guarantee, at the database level, what your serverless architecture aims to ensure at the ecosystem level.

You're building a glorified database for your web and mobile apps :)

87 https://en.wikipedia.org/wiki/ACID
88 https://serverlesshandbook.dev/serverless-architecture-principles

Types of databases

You can classify databases into 4 categories based on how they prioritize opposing optimization criteria.

1. **Flat file storage** the simplest and fastest solution, great for large data
2. **Relational databases** the most correct and surprisingly fast solution, great for complex data
3. **NoSQL** the class of databases breaking ACID for greater speed/scalability; different types exist
4. **Blockchain** a distributed database without a central authority, the industry is figuring out what it's good for

Regardless of what you choose, you will talk to your database through the network. It runs on a different machine.

The network round-trips are a bottomline performance limit. No matter how fast your database, you can't get data faster than it can fly through the network.

Serverless providers optimize by running your code as close to your database as possible. If that's not enough, you'll have to run your own servers.

Flat file database

The simplest way to store data is a flat file database[89] . You might call it "organized files".

Flat files are commonly used for blobby binary data like images. You'll want to put them on S3 for a serverless environment. That negates some of the advantages.

Advantages of flat files

Compared to other databases, flat files have zero overhead. Your data goes straight to storage without database logic.

89 https://en.wikipedia.org/wiki/Flat-file_database

This creates amazing read and write performance. As long as you're adding data to the end of a file, creating a new file, and reading the file start to finish.

A good naming structure gives you fast access to specific files.

Disadvantages of flat files

Flat files struggle with updates.

To add a line at the beginning of a file, you have to move the whole thing. To change a line in the middle, you have to update everything that comes after.

There's no query interface either. You have to read your files to compare, analyze, and search. And without a database, there's no ACID or data shape guarantees.

When should you store data in flat files

Flat file storage is great when you're looking for speed and simplicity.

Use flat files when:

1. You need fast append-only writes

2. You have simple querying requirements
3. You read data more often than you write data
4. You write data that you rarely read

Avoid flat files when:

1. You need to cross-reference data or use complex queries
2. You need fast access across your entire database
3. Your data changes a lot

No. 3 is the flat file database killer.

Common use cases for flat files are logs, large datasets, and binary files (image, video, etc).

Read about how to use flat files in the appendix[90]

---

90   https://serverlesshandbook.dev/appendix-more-databases#
flat-file-database

Relational databases – RDBMS

Relational databases[91] are the most common type of database. Data lives in a structured data model and many features exist to optimize performance.

Choosing a relational database for your business data is almost always the right decision.

Advantages of relational databases

Relational databases have been around since the 1970's. They're battle tested, reliable, and can adapt to almost any workload.

91 https://en.wikipedia.org/wiki/Relational_database

Modern systems incorporate popular features from NoSQL like unstructured JSON data. Postgres[92] even outperforms NoSQL solutions on certain performance benchmarks.

The defining feature of relational databases is the relational data model which lets you model complex data using small isolated concepts. You almost always end up reimplementing this idea with other databases.

And after decades of research, relational databases are *fast*.

Disadvantages of relational databases

Relational databases are harder to use, require more expertise to tune performance, and you lose flexibility. This can be a good thing.

You can create a database that's fast as lightning, reach a magic number of entries, and performance falls off a cliff. It's hard to horizontally scale a relational database.

But you *can* make it more flexible with a blobby JSON field on every model. Perfect for metadata.

When to store data in a relational DB

Choosing a relational database is almost always the correct choice.

92 https://en.wikipedia.org/wiki/PostgreSQL

Use relational DBs when:

1. You don't know how you're using your data
2. You benefit from data integrity
3. You need good performance up to hundreds of millions of entries
4. Your app fits in a single data center (availability zone)
5. You often use different objects together

Avoid relational DBs when:

1. You're storing binary data (images, video)
2. You don't care about data integrity
3. You don't want to invest in initial setup
4. You just need a quick way to save something
5. You have more data than fits on 1 server

This makes relational databases the perfect choice for typical applications. You wouldn't use an RDBMS for files, but should consider it for metadata about those files.

Read about how to use relational databases in the appendix[93]

93   https://serverlesshandbook.dev/appendix-more-databases# relational-databases--rdbms

The NoSQL approach

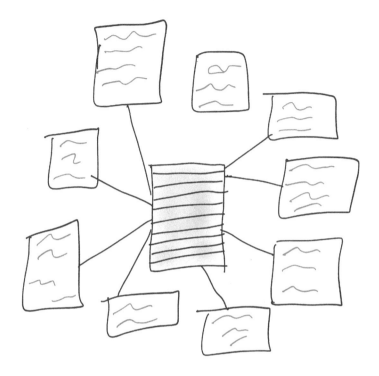

"NoSQL" represents a broad range of technologies built for different reasons. A catch-all for any database that isn't relational.

Flat files are a type of NoSQL database.

Wikipedia offers a great description[94] :

94 https://en.wikipedia.org/wiki/NoSQL

The data structures used by NoSQL databases are different from those used by default in relational databases, making some operations faster in NoSQL. The particular suitability of a given NoSQL database depends on the problem it must solve.

This variety is where NoSQL shines. Where relational databases aim to fit many use cases, NoSQL solutions aim to solve a specific problem.

Flavors of NoSQL

You can classify NoSQL databases in 4 categories:

1. **key:value store** works like a dictionary. A unique key points to a stored value. Fast read/write performance makes this an ideal caching layer in front of a relational database.
2. **document store** maps unique keys to documents. Like key:value stores with complex values. Many come with a great query engine.
3. **graph database** store graph data structures efficiently. Useful for domains with many circular references like social connections and road maps.
4. **wide column database** act as a mix between a document store and a relational database. Keys map to objects that fit a schema, but the schema isn't prescriptive.

Typical modern databases support multiple models.

Which NoSQL flavor should you pick?

It depends. What are you trying to do?

I would prioritize a managed database solution from my serverless provider. Cuts down on networking overhead and makes your life easier because there's one less thing to manage.

Then I would pick what fits my use case.

Use key:value stores when you need blazing fast data with low overhead.

Use a document DB or wide column store when you want a generic database that isn't relational.

Use a graph DB when you're storing graph data.

My favorite advantage of NoSQL databases is the wonderful integration with the JavaScript/TypeScript ecosystem. Store JSON blobs, read JavaScript objects.

Disadvantages of NoSQL databases

Disadvantages of NoSQL stem from its advantages. Funny how that works.

The simplicity of key:value stores gives you speed at the cost of not being able to store complex data.

The write speed of document databases comes at the cost of ACID compliance. Often using the eventual consistency[95] model to write fast and distribute later.

The ease of schema-less development comes at the cost of inconsistent data. NoSQL databases tend to struggle with relations between objects. You can do it, but feels clunky.

Read more about choosing a NoSQL database and how to use it in the appendix[96]

Blockchain

Blockchain is the new kid on the block. Mixed up with cryptocurrencies and financial speculation, it's a solid way to share and store data.

95 https://en.wikipedia.org/wiki/Eventual_consistency
96   https://serverlesshandbook.dev/appendix-more-databases#
the-nosql-approach-to-data

You've used one before 👉 git.

That's right, git[97] and The Blockchain[98] share the same underlying data structure: a merkle tree.

A merkle tree[99] stores data in a cryptographically verified sequence of blocks. Each block contains a cryptographic hash of the previous block, which means you can verify the whole chain.

As a result you don't need a central authority to tell you the current state of your data. Each client can decide, if their data is valid.

Adding a consensus algorithm makes the process even more robust. When you add new data, how many servers have to agree that the data is valid?

The result is a slow, but robustly decentralized database.

I wouldn't use the blockchain in production just yet, but it's an exciting space to watch. Blockstack[100] is a great way to start.

---

97 https://en.wikipedia.org/wiki/Git
98 https://en.wikipedia.org/wiki/Blockchain
99 https://en.wikipedia.org/wiki/Merkle_tree
100 https://blockstack.org/

What should you choose?

Projects tend to use a combination of database technologies.

Files for large binary blobs, relational database for business data, key:value store for persistent caching, document store for complex data that lives together.

Adding JSON blobs to relational data is a common compromise. 🤏

Next chapter, we look at building a RESTful API for your data.

Creating a REST API

You've heard of REST before, but what *is* REST? How does it work? Can you build one from scratch? Does serverless make your REST life easier?

In this chapter, learn about REST best practices and finish with a small implementation you can try right now. I left mine running ✌️

What is REST

REST[101] stands for REpresentational State Transfer. Coined in Roy Fielding's 2000 doctoral thesis[102], it now represents the standard approach to web APIs.

Fielding says REST is an architectural principle. It *recommends* how to build a scalable web system, but there's no official standard.

You may have noticed this in the wild. RESTful APIs follow similar guidelines and no two are alike.

These days any API that uses HTTP to transfer data and URLs to identify resources is called REST.

Here are the 6 architectural constraints that define a RESTful system 👇

- **client-server architecture** specifies a separation of concerns between the user interface and the storage

101 https://en.wikipedia.org/wiki/Representational_state_transfer
102 https://www.ics.uci.edu/~fielding/pubs/dissertation/top.htm

of data. This simplifies both sides and lets them evolve independently.

- **statelessness** specifies that *the protocol* is stateless. Each request to the server contains all information necessary to process that request. Servers do not maintain client context.
- **cacheability** specifies that clients can cache any server response to improve performance on future requests. Servers have to annotate responses with appropriate caching policies via http headers
- **layered system** means that, like regular HTTP, a RESTful client shouldn't need to know whether it's talking to a server, a proxy, or load balancer. This improves scalability.
- **code on demand (optional)** says that servers can send executable code as part of their responses. You see this with web servers sending JavaScript.
- **uniform interface** is the most fundamental and means that clients can interact with a server purely from responses, without outside knowledge.

A uniform interface

Creating a uniform interface is the most important aspect of a RESTful API. The less clients know about your server, the better.

Each **request identifies the resource** it is requesting. Using the URL itself.

Responses send a representation of a resource rather than the resource itself. Like compiling a set of database objects into a JSON document.

All **messages are self-descriptive** meaning both client and server can understand a message without external information. Send everything you need.

A resource's **representation includes everything needed to modify** that resource. When clients get a response, it should contain everything necessary to modify or delete the underlying resources.

Academics say **responses should list possible actions** so clients can navigate a system without intimate knowledge of its API. You rarely see this in the wild.

Designing a RESTful API

The trickiest part of building a RESTful API is how it evolves over time. The second trickiest is keeping it consistent across your app.

As your system grows you're tempted to piggy-back on existing APIs and break resource constraints. You're likely to forget the exact wording and phrasing of different parts.

All that is natural. **The important part is to start on the right foot and clean up when you can.**

Engineers are human

When engineers *can* do something with your API, they will.

They're going to find every undocumented feature, discover every "alternative" way to get data and uncover any easter egg you didn't mean to include. They're good at their job.

Do yourself a favor and aim to **keep everything consistent**. The more consistent you are, the easier it will be to clean up.

That means

- all dates in the same format
- all responses in the same shape
- keep field types consistent, if an error is a string it's always a string
- include every field name and value in full
- when multiple endpoints include the same model, make it *the same*

Here are tips I've picked up over the past 14 years of building and using RESTful APIs.

URL schema

Your URL schema exists to solve *one* problem: Create a uniform way to identify resources and endpoints on your server.

Keep it consistent, otherwise don't sweat it.

Engineers like to get stuck on pointless details, but it's okay. Make sure your team agrees on what makes sense.

When designing a URL schema I aim to:

- **make it guessable**, which stems from consistency and predictability
- **make it human readable**, which makes it easier to use, debug, and memorize
- **avoid query strings** because they look messy and can make copy paste debugging harder
- **avoid strange characters** like spaces and emojis. It looks cute, but it's cumbersome to work with
- **include IDs in URLs** because it makes debugging and logging easier

The two schemas I like, go like this:

```
https://api.wonderfulservice.com/<namespace>/
        <model>/<id>
```

Using an `api.*` subdomain helps with load balancing and using special servers for your API. **Less** relevant in the serverless world because providers create unique domains.

The optional <namespace> helps you stay organized. As your app grows, you'll notice different areas use similar-sounding names.

You don't need a namespace for generic models like `user` or `subscription`.

Adding a `<model>` that's named after the model on your backend helps you stay sane. Yes it breaks the idea of total separation between client and server, but it's useful to maintain consistency.

If everyone calls everything the same name, you never need to translate. 😅

The `<id>` identifies the specific instance of a model that you're changing.

Sometimes it's useful to use this alternative schema:

```
https://api.wonderfulservice.com/<namespace>/
        <model>/<verb>/<id>
```

The verb specifies what you're doing to the model. More on that when we discuss HTTP verbs further down.

Data format

Use JSON. Both for sending data and for receiving data.

Great support in common programming languages, easy to use with JavaScript, simple to write by hand, readable by humans, not verbose. That makes JSON the perfect format for a modern API.

For timestamps I recommend the ISO 8601 standard[103] for the same reason. Great tooling in all languages, readable by humans, writable by hand.

UNIX timestamps[104] used to be popular and are falling out of favor. Hard to read for humans, don't work great with dates beyond 2038, bad at dates before 1970.

Stick to ISO time and JSON data 😊

Using HTTP verbs

Verbs specify *what* your request does with a resource.

Opinions on how to pass verbs from client to server vary. There's 3 camps:

1. stick to HTTP verbs
2. verbs belong in the URL

103 https://en.wikipedia.org/wiki/ISO_8601
104 https://en.wikipedia.org/wiki/Unix_time

3. verbs are part of the JSON payload

Everyone agrees that a GET request is for getting data and should have no side-effects.

Other verbs belong to the POST request. Or you can use HTTP verbs like PUT, PATCH, and DELETE.

I like to use a combination.

GET for getting data. POST for posting data (both create and update). DELETE for deleting ... on the rare occasion I let clients delete data.

PUT and PATCH can be frustrating to work with in client libraries.

Errors

Should you use HTTP error codes to communicate errors?

Opinions vary.

One camp says that HTTP errors are for HTTP-layer problems. Your server being down, a bad URL, invalid payload, etc. When your application processes a request and decides there's an error, it should return 200 with an error object.

The other camp says that's silly and we already have a great system for errors. Your application should use the full gamut of HTTP error codes *and return an error object.*

Always return a descriptive JSON error object. That's a given. Make sure your server doesn't return HTML when there's an error.

An error shape like:

```
{
  "status": "error",
  "error": "This is what went wrong"
}
```

is best.

I like to combine both approaches. 500 errors for my application failing to do its job, 404 for things that aren't found, 200 with an explanation for everything else. Helps avoid hunting for obscure error codes and sticks to the basics of HTTP.

Added bonus: You can read the error object. Will you remember what error 418 means?

Versioning

I have given up on versioning APIs.

Your best bet is to maintain eternal backwards compatibility. Make additive changes when needed, remove things never.

It leads to messy APIs, which is a shame, but better than crashing an app the user hasn't updated in 3 years.

When you need a breaking change, it's unlikely the underlying model fits your current URL schema. Use a new URL.

Build a simple REST

To show you how this works in practice, we're going to build a serverless REST API. Accepts and returns JSON blobs, stores them in DynamoDB.

You can see the full code on GitHub[105] . I encourage you to play around and try deploying to your own AWS.

Code samples here are excerpts.

URL schema mapped to Lambdas

We start with a URL schema and lambda function definitions in `serverless.yml`.

---

105   https://github.com/Swizec/serverlesshandbook.dev/tree/master/
examples/serverless-rest-example

```yaml
# serverless.yml

functions:
  getItems:
    handler: dist/manageItems.getItem
    events:
      - http:
          path: item/{itemId}
          method: GET
          cors: true
  updateItems:
    handler: dist/manageItems.updateItem
    events:
      - http:
          path: item
          method: POST
          cors: true
      - http:
          path: item/{itemId}
          method: POST
          cors: true
  deleteItems:
    handler: dist/manageItems.deleteItem
    events:
      - http:
          path: item/{itemId}
          method: DELETE
          cors: true
```

This defines the 4 operations of a basic CRUD app:

- `getItem` to fetch items
- `updateItem` to create items
- `updateItem/id` to update items
- `deleteItem` to delete items

The `{itemId}` syntax lets APIGateway parse the URL for us and pass identifiers to our code as parameters.

Mapping every operation to its own lambda means you don't have to write routing code. When a lambda gets called, it knows what to do.

We define lambdas in a `manageItems.ts` file[106] . Grouping operations from the same model helps keep your code organized.

getItem

```
// src/manageItems.ts

// fetch using /item/ID
export const getItem = async (event: APIGatewayEvent):
↪   Promise<APIResponse> => {
```

---

106   https://github.com/Swizec/serverlesshandbook.dev/blob/master/
examples/serverless-rest-example/src/manageItems.ts

```
const itemId = event.pathParameters ?
↳  event.pathParameters.itemId : ""

const item = await db.getItem({
  TableName: process.env.ITEM_TABLE!,
  Key: { itemId },
})

if (item.Item) {
  return response(200, {
    status: "success",
    item: item.Item,
  })
} else {
  return response(404, {
    status: "error",
    error: "Item not found",
  })
}
}
```

The getItem function is triggered from an API Gateway Event. It includes a pathParameters object that contains an itemId parsed from the URL.

We then use a DynamoDB getItem wrapper[107] to talk to the database and find the requested item.

107   https://github.com/Swizec/serverlesshandbook.dev/blob/master/
examples/serverless-rest-example/src/dynamodb.ts#L80

If the item is found, we return a success response, otherwise an error. The response method is a helper that makes responses easier to write.

```
// src/manageItems.ts

function response(statusCode: number, body: any) {
  return {
    statusCode,
    body: JSON.stringify(body),
  }
}
```

You can try it out in your terminal like this:

```
curl https://4sklrwb1jg.execute-api.us-east-1.amazonaws.com/\
    dev/item/0769413a-b306-46cb-a03c-5a8d5e29aa3e
```

Or go to serverlesshandbook.dev/claim to access interactive features.

updateItem

Updating an item is the most complex operation we've got.

It handles both creating and updating items, always assuming that the client knows best. You'll want to validate that in production.

Here we overwrite server data with the client payload.

```
// upsert an item
// /item or /item/ID
export const updateItem = async (
  event: APIGatewayEvent
): Promise<APIResponse> => {
  let itemId = event.pathParameters ?
↪   event.pathParameters.itemId : uuidv4()

  let createdAt = new Date().toISOString()

  if (event.pathParameters && \
    event.pathParameters.itemId) {
    // find item if exists
    const find = await db.getItem({
      TableName: process.env.ITEM_TABLE!,
      Key: { itemId },
    })
    if (find.Item) {
      // save createdAt so we don't overwrite on update
      createdAt = find.Item.createdAt
    } else {
      return response(404, {
        status: "error",
```

```
      error: "Item not found",
    })
  }
}

if (!event.body) {
  return response(400, {
    status: "error",
    error: "Provide a JSON body",
  })
}

let body = JSON.parse(event.body)

if (body.itemId) {
  // this will confuse DynamoDB, you can't update the key
  delete body.itemId
}

const item = await db.updateItem({
  TableName: process.env.ITEM_TABLE!,
  Key: { itemId },
  UpdateExpression: `SET ${db.buildExpression(
    body
  )}, createdAt = :createdAt, lastUpdatedAt =
↪   :lastUpdatedAt`,
  ExpressionAttributeValues: {
    ...db.buildAttributes(body),
    ":createdAt": createdAt,
    ":lastUpdatedAt": new Date().toISOString(),
  },
  ReturnValues: "ALL_NEW",
```

```
  })

  return response(200, {
    status: "success",
    item: item.Attributes,
  })
}
```

The pattern we're following is:

- if no ID provided, generate one
- find item in DB
- update or create a createdAt timestamp
- parse the JSON body
- create an update expression
- add a lastUpdatedAt timestamp
- return the resulting object

Adding createdAt and lastUpdatedAt timestamps is helpful when debugging these systems. You want to know when something happened.

You can find the db.* helper methods in my dynamodb.ts file[108]

You can try it out in your terminal like this:

108 https://github.com/Swizec/serverlesshandbook.dev/blob/master/
examples/serverless-rest-example/src/dynamodb.ts

```
curl -d '{"hello_world": "this is a json item", \
"params": "It can have multiple params", \
"customNumber": 4}' \
https://4sklrwb1jg.execute-api.us-east-1.amazonaws.com/\
dev/item
```

To create an item.

```
curl -d '{"hello_world": "this is a json item",\
"params": "It can have multiple params", \
"customNumber": 4}' \
https://4sklrwb1jg.execute-api.us-east-1.amazonaws.com/dev/\
item/e76e46f4-296d-4fef-a349-a1bb5717f2ac
```

To update an item.

Or go to serverlesshandbook.dev/claim to access interactive features.

deleteItem

Deleting is easy by comparison. Get the ID, delete the item. With no verification that you should or shouldn't be able to.

```typescript
// src/manageItems.ts

export const deleteItem = async (
  event: APIGatewayEvent
): Promise<APIResponse> => {
  const itemId = event.pathParameters ?
  ↪  event.pathParameters.itemId : null

  if (!itemId) {
    return response(400, {
      status: "error",
      error: "Provide an itemId",
    })
  }

  // DynamoDB handles deleting already deleted values,
    // no error :)
  const item = await db.deleteItem({
    TableName: process.env.ITEM_TABLE!,
    Key: { itemId },
    ReturnValues: "ALL_OLD",
  })

  return response(200, {
    status: "success",
    itemWas: item.Attributes,
  })
}
```

We get itemId from the URL props and call a deleteItem method on DynamoDB. The API returns the item as it was before deletion.

PS: in a production system you'll want to use soft deletes – mark as deleted and keep the data

Fin ✌️

And that's 14 years of REST API experience condensed into 2000 words. My favorite is how much easier this is to implement using serverless than with Rails or Express.

I love that you can have different lambda functions (whole servers, really) for individual endpoints.

Next chapter, we look at GraphQL and why it represents an exciting future.

Serverless GraphQL API

Say you're building an app. It needs data from a server. What do you do?

You make a fetch() request.

```
fetch("https://swapi.dev/api/people/1/")
    .then((res) => res.json())
    .then(console.log)
```

And you get eeeevery piece of info about Luke Skywalker.

```
{
    "name": "Luke Skywalker",
    "height": "172",
    "mass": "77",
    "hair_color": "blond",
    "skin_color": "fair",
    "eye_color": "blue",
    "birth_year": "19BBY",
    "gender": "male",
    "homeworld": "https://swapi.dev/api/planets/1/",
    "films": [
        "https://swapi.dev/api/films/2/",
```

```
    "https://swapi.dev/api/films/6/",
    "https://swapi.dev/api/films/3/",
    "https://swapi.dev/api/films/1/",
    "https://swapi.dev/api/films/7/"
  ],
  "species": ["https://swapi.dev/api/species/1/"],
  "vehicles": [
    "https://swapi.dev/api/vehicles/14/",
    "https://swapi.dev/api/vehicles/30/"
  ],
  "starships": [
    "https://swapi.dev/api/starships/12/",
    "https://swapi.dev/api/starships/22/"
  ],
  "created": "2014-12-09T13:50:51.644000Z",
  "edited": "2014-12-20T21:17:56.891000Z",
  "url": "https://swapi.dev/api/people/1/"
}
```

Frustrating ... all you wanted was his name and hair color. Why's the API sending you all this crap? 🗿

And what's this about Luke's species being 1? What the heck is 1?

You make another fetch request.

```
fetch("https://swapi.dev/api/species/1/")
  .then((res) => res.json())
  .then(console.log)
```

You get data about humans. Great.

```
{
  "name": "Human",
  "classification": "mammal",
  "designation": "sentient",
  "average_height": "180",
  "skin_colors": "caucasian, black, asian, hispanic",
  "hair_colors": "blonde, brown, black, red",
  "eye_colors": "brown, blue, green, hazel, grey, amber",
  "average_lifespan": "120",
  "homeworld": "https://swapi.dev/api/planets/9/",
  "language": "Galactic Basic",
  "people": [
    "https://swapi.dev/api/people/1/",
    "https://swapi.dev/api/people/4/",
    "https://swapi.dev/api/people/5/",
    "https://swapi.dev/api/people/6/",
    "https://swapi.dev/api/people/7/",
    "https://swapi.dev/api/people/9/",
```

```
    "https://swapi.dev/api/people/10/",
    "https://swapi.dev/api/people/11/",
    "https://swapi.dev/api/people/12/",
    "https://swapi.dev/api/people/14/",
    "https://swapi.dev/api/people/18/",
    "https://swapi.dev/api/people/19/",
    "https://swapi.dev/api/people/21/",
    "https://swapi.dev/api/people/22/",
    "https://swapi.dev/api/people/25/",
    "https://swapi.dev/api/people/26/",
    "https://swapi.dev/api/people/28/",
    "https://swapi.dev/api/people/29/",
    "https://swapi.dev/api/people/32/",
    "https://swapi.dev/api/people/34/",
    "https://swapi.dev/api/people/43/",
    "https://swapi.dev/api/people/51/",
    "https://swapi.dev/api/people/60/",
    "https://swapi.dev/api/people/61/",
    "https://swapi.dev/api/people/62/",
    "https://swapi.dev/api/people/66/",
    "https://swapi.dev/api/people/67/",
    "https://swapi.dev/api/people/68/",
    "https://swapi.dev/api/people/69/",
    "https://swapi.dev/api/people/74/",
    "https://swapi.dev/api/people/81/",
    "https://swapi.dev/api/people/84/",
    "https://swapi.dev/api/people/85/",
    "https://swapi.dev/api/people/86/",
    "https://swapi.dev/api/people/35/"
  ],
  "films": [
    "https://swapi.dev/api/films/2/",
```

```
      "https://swapi.dev/api/films/7/",
      "https://swapi.dev/api/films/5/",
      "https://swapi.dev/api/films/4/",
      "https://swapi.dev/api/films/6/",
      "https://swapi.dev/api/films/3/",
      "https://swapi.dev/api/films/1/"
   ],
   "created": "2014-12-10T13:52:11.567000Z",
   "edited": "2015-04-17T06:59:55.850671Z",
   "url": "https://swapi.dev/api/species/1/"
}
```

That's a lot of JSON to get the word "Human" out of the Star Wars
API[109] ...

109 https://swapi.dev/

What about Luke's starships? There's 2 and that means 2 more API requests ...

```
fetch("https://swapi.dev/api/starships/12/")
  .then((res) => res.json())
  .then(console.log)

fetch("https://swapi.dev/api/starships/22/")
  .then((res) => res.json())
  .then(console.log)
```

Wanna know how much JSON that dumps? Try a guess. 🙄

You made **4 API requests** and transferred a bunch of data to find out that Luke Skywalker is human, has blond hair, and flies an X-Wing and an Imperial Shuttle.

And guess what, you didn't cache anything. How often do you think this data changes? Once a year? Twice?

🙇

GraphQL to the rescue

Here's what the same process looks like with GraphQL.

```
query luke {
  // id found through allPeople query
  person(id: "cGVvcGxlOjE=") {
    name
    name
    hairColor
    species {
      name
    }
    starshipConnection {
      starships {
        name
      }
    }
  }
}
```

And the API returns what you wanted with 1 request.

```
{
  "data": {
    "person": {
      "name": "Luke Skywalker",
      "hairColor": "blond",
      "species": null,
      "starshipConnection": {
        "starships": [
          {
            "name": "X-wing"
          },
          {
            "name": "Imperial shuttle"
          }
        ]
      }
    }
  }
}
```

An API mechanism that gives you flexibility on the frontend, slashes API requests, *and doesn't transfer data you don't need?*

Write a query, say what you want, send to an endpoint, GraphQL figures out the rest. Want different params? Just say so. Want multiple models? Got it. Wanna go deep? You can.

Without changes on the server. Within reason.

GraphQL client libraries can add caching to avoid duplicate requests. And because queries are structured, clients can merge queries into 1 API call.

I fell in love the moment it clicked.

You can try it on graphql.org's public playground[110]

What *is* GraphQL

GraphQL[111] is an open-source data query and manipulation language for APIs and a runtime for fulfilling queries with existing data.

Touted as a replacement for REST, GraphQL is actually a different approach to APIs. Better for common use-cases and with its own drawbacks.

110 http://graphql.org/swapi-graphql
111 https://en.wikipedia.org/wiki/GraphQL

Don't let the propaganda fool you 👉 you can and *should* use both REST *and* GraphQL. Depends on what you're doing.

GraphQL's benefit is its declarative nature.

On the client, you describe the shape of what you want and GraphQL figures it out. On the server, you write resolver functions for sub-queries and GraphQL combines them into the full result.

REST queries can be declarative on the client, while GraphQL is declarative on both ends. For reads *and* writes.

GraphQL queries

GraphQL queries fetch data. Following this pattern:

```
query {
  what_you_want {
    its_property
  }
}
```

You nest fields – representing your models – and properties into queries to describe what you're looking for. You can go as deep as you want.

Write fields side-by-side to execute multiple queries with a single API request.

```
query {
  what_you_want {
    its_property
  }
  other_thing_you_want {
    its_property {
      property_of_property
    }
  }
}
```

This is where the power and flexibility come from.

Variables let you create dynamic queries and build complex filters to limit the scope of your result.

```
query queryName($filterProp: "value") {
    field(filterProp: $filterProp) {
        property1
        property3
    }
}
```

$filterProp defines a new variable that the field() lookup uses to filter results for those matching "value".

GraphQL comes with basic equality filters built-in and you're encouraged to add more in your resolvers. Typical projects choose to support sorting, greater-than, not-equals, etc.

GraphQL mutations

GraphQL mutations write data. Following this pattern:

```
mutation {
  what_youre_updating(argument: "value", argument2: "val
↪  2") {
    prop_you_want_back
```

```
        }
    }
```

Like a query with arguments, you specify what you're updating and pass your values. What's available depends on how mutation resolvers are implemented on the server.

The mutation body specifies what you'd like returned. Same as a query.

Like queries, you can put mutations side-by-side and use variables.

```
mutation mutationName($argument: "value") {
    what_youre_updating(argument: $argument) {
        prop_you_want_back
    }

    other_field(argument: $argument) {
        return_prop
    }
}
```

GraphQL vs. REST, which to use and when

The GraphQL vs. REST debate is a false dichotomy.

People like to say GraphQL is *replacing* REST and that's not the case. GraphQL is *augmenting* REST.

Will GraphQL become the default API layer? It might.

Should you rip out your REST API and rewrite for GraphQL? Please don't.

GraphQL doesn't care where data comes from. Relational database, NoSQL database, files, a REST API, another GraphQL API ... All you need is a function that reads data in response to a query.

You can start using GraphQL without changing your existing server[112] with a GraphQL middle layer. Create a GraphQL server on top of your REST API.

112 https://bit.ly/3sxq4Vn

How do you choose between REST and GraphQL?

When building a typical CRUD – Create, Read, Update, Delete – API, I like to ask 6 questions:

1. Is this a new project? *Default to GraphQL*
2. Do I know in advance what clients are going to need? *REST is great*
3. Am I fetching small subsets of large data? *GraphQL*
4. Am I generating new values for each request? *REST*
5. Updating a few properties on an object? *GraphQL*
6. Submitting large payloads to be saved? *REST*

Use upserts to deal with Create and Update. Avoid deletes.

Should you expose your entire data model verbatim?

No.

Exposing your full data model is a common mistake in API design.

Define a clean API using domain driven design[113]. How your back-end stores data for max performance and good database design differs from how clients think about that data.

113 https://en.wikipedia.org/wiki/Domain-driven_design

Figure 0.4: Example create mutation from server below

An "access to everything" API style is hard to use, leads to security issues, is difficult to maintain, and tightly couples servers and clients. You'll have to update both server and client for any DB change.

Then there's the question of derived and computed properties with complex business logic. You don't want to re-implement those on the client using raw data from your database.

How to create a serverless GraphQL server

There's many ways to build a GraphQL server, the nicest I've found is with Apollo[114] 's apollo-server-lambda[115] package.

You follow a 4 step process:

1. Add lambda to your `serverless.yml` file
2. Initialize the Apollo server
3. Specify your schema
4. Add resolvers

We created a small REST API[116] in the previous chapter, let's recreate it with GraphQL. Full code on GitHub[117]

Apollo creates a GraphQL playground for us. You can try my implementation here:

```
https://yrqqg5l31m.execute-api.us-east-1.amazonaws.com/\
    dev/graphql
```

Or go to serverlesshandbook.dev/claim to access interactive features.

114 https://www.apollographql.com/
115   https://github.com/apollographql/apollo-server/tree/master/packages/
apollo-server-lambda
116 https://serverlesshandbook.dev/serverless-rest- api#build-a-simple-rest
117   https://github.com/Swizec/serverlesshandbook.dev/tree/master/
examples/serverless-graphql-example

serverless.yml

We define a new function in the `functions:` section.

```
# serverless.yml

functions:
  graphql:
    handler: dist/graphql.handler
    events:
      - http:
          path: graphql
          method: GET
          cors: true
      - http:
          path: graphql
          method: POST
          cors: true
```

The convention is to use the `/graphql` endpoint for everything.

Make sure to define both GET and POST endpoints. GET serves the Apollo playground, POST handles the queries and mutations.

initialize Apollo server

Every Apollo server needs a schema, a resolvers object, and the initialized server. Like this:

```
// src/graphql.ts

import { ApolloServer, gql } from "apollo-server-lambda"

// this is where we define the shape of our API
const schema = gql``

// this is where the shape maps to functions
const resolvers = {
  Query: {},
  Mutation: {},
}

const server = new ApolloServer({ typeDefs: schema,
↪  resolvers })

export const handler = server.createHandler({
  cors: {
    // for security in production, lock this to your real
    ↪  URLs
    origin: "*",
```

```
    credentials: true,
  },
})
```

This server won't run because the `schema` and `resolvers` don't match. Resolvers have fields that the schema does not.

We'll add type definitions to the schema and a resolver for each `Query` and `Mutation`.

specify your schema

Your schema defines the shape of your API. Every type of object your server returns and every query and mutation definition.

You get a type-safe API because GraphQL ensures objects follow this schema. Both when coming into the API and when flying out.

To mimic our CRUD API from before[118] , we use a schema like this:

```
// src/graphql.ts

const schema = gql`
```

118 https://serverlesshandbook.dev/serverless-rest-api#build-a-simple-rest

```
type Item {
  id: String
  name: String
  body: String
  createdAt: String
  updatedAt: String
}

type Query {
  item(id: String!): Item
}

type Mutation {
  updateItem(id: String, name: String, body: String):
↪   Item
  deleteItem(id: String!): Item
}
`
```

With REST, users could store and retrieve arbitrary JSON blobs.
GraphQL doesn't support that. Instead, we define an Item type
with an arbitrary body string.

You can use that to store serialized JSON objects.

Each item will have an id, a name, and a few timestamps managed
by the server. Those help with debugging.

Our item() query lets you retrieve items and requires an id to
work. That's the exclamation point after String.

Then we have a mutation for upserting items and a mutation for deleting.

create your resolvers

We have 1 query and 2 mutations. That means we'll need 3 resolver functions.

We can copy these from the REST implementation[119] and change how we get arguments.

I like to put queries in a `src/queries.ts` file and mutations in a `src/mutations.ts`. You can organize this by model as your implementation grows.

item()

The `item()` query is a basic fetch and looks like this:

```
// src/queries.ts

import * as db from "simple-dynamodb"
```

119 https://serverlesshandbook.dev/serverless-rest-api#build-a-simple-rest

```
function remapProps(item: any) {
  return {
    ...item,
    id: item.itemId,
    name: item.itemName,
  }
}


// fetch using item(id: String)
export const item = async (_: any, args: { id: string }) =>
↪ {
  const item = await db.getItem({
    TableName: process.env.ITEM_TABLE!,
    Key: {
      itemId: args.id,
    },
  })

  return remapProps(item.Item)
}
```

We can ignore Apollo's first resolver argument. The second argument is where query and mutation values come in.

Since id is a required param, you don't have to check for nulls. GraphQL handles that before calling your resolver.

You can call getItem on DynamoDB, or run a SQL query for a relational database, and return the result. GraphQL handles the rest.

One niggle to note ☞ DynamoDB considers name and id reserved attributes. We remap them to itemName and itemId when saving and have to map them back to pretty GraphQL attributes when reading.

This is what I meant by *"You don't want to expose raw database details to your API"* :)

updateItem()

The updateItem() mutation is our upsert.

It creates a new item when you don't send an id and updates the existing item when you do. If no item is found, the mutation throws an error.

And it handles createdAt and updatedAt timestamps.

```
// src/mutations.ts

type ItemArgs = {
  id: string
  name: string
  body: string
}
```

```
// upsert an item
// item(name, ...) or item(id, name, ...)
export const updateItem = async (_: any, args: ItemArgs) =>
↪ {
  let itemId = args.id ? args.id : uuidv4()

  let createdAt = new Date().toISOString()

  // find item if exists
  if (args.id) {
    const find = await db.getItem({
      TableName: process.env.ITEM_TABLE!,
      Key: { itemId },
    })

    if (find.Item) {
      // save createdAt so we don't overwrite on update
      createdAt = find.Item.createdAt
    } else {
      throw "Item not found"
    }
  }

  const updateValues = {
    itemName: args.name,
    body: args.body,
  }

  const item = await db.updateItem({
    TableName: process.env.ITEM_TABLE!,
    Key: { itemId },
    UpdateExpression: `SET ${db.buildExpression(
```

```
      updateValues
    )}, createdAt = :createdAt, updatedAt = :updatedAt`,
    ExpressionAttributeValues: {
      ...db.buildAttributes(updateValues),
      ":createdAt": createdAt,
      ":updatedAt": new Date().toISOString(),
    },
    ReturnValues: "ALL_NEW",
  })

  return remapProps(item.Attributes)
}
```

We take the id from arguments or create a new one with uuidv4().

Then we try to find the item.

If found, we change createdAt to the existing value. Otherwise we throw an error. That helps you avoid creating new items by accident because DynamoDB always upserts.

We define the updateValues and build a DynamoDB UPDATE query. This can look gnarly no matter what DB you use.

In the end, we return the object our database returned and let GraphQL handle the rest.

deleteItem()

The deleteItem() mutation is simple. GraphQL and the database do the work for us.

```
// src/mutations.ts

export const deleteItem = async (_: any, args: { id: string
↪ }) => {
  // DynamoDB handles deleting already deleted objects, no
  ↪ error :)
  const item = await db.deleteItem({
    TableName: process.env.ITEM_TABLE!,
    Key: {
      itemId: args.id,
    },
    ReturnValues: "ALL_OLD",
  })

  return remapProps(item.Attributes)
}
```

We take the id from mutation arguments, ask our database to delete the row, and return the old attributes.

add resolvers to the GraphQL server

We built the resolvers, now we add them to `graphql.ts`:

```
// src/graphql.ts

import { item } from "./queries"
import { updateItem, deleteItem } from "./mutations"

// ...

const resolvers = {
  Query: {
    item,
  },
  Mutation: {
    updateItem,
    deleteItem,
  },
}
```

This tells Apollo how to map queries and mutations to resolvers. We can use generic names because this is a small project.

You'll want to namespace in bigger apps.

Try it out

Run `yarn deploy` and you get a GraphQL server. There's even an Apollo playground that helps you test.

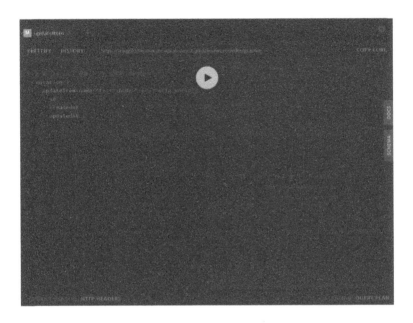

Try mine at:

```
https://yrqqg5l3lm.execute-api.us-east-1.amazonaws.com/\
dev/graphql
```

or go to serverlesshandbook.dev/claim to access interactive features.

GraphQL no-code services

Wiring up GraphQL can get tedious with lots of repetitive code.

Various no-code and low-code solutions exist that do the work for you. Look at your database and magic a GraphQL server into existence.

They tend to exhibit the *expose entire DB as API* problem. But they can be a good starting point.

Next chapter we look at building lambda pipelines for distributed data processing.

Lambda pipelines for serverless data processing

You get tens of thousands of events per hour. How do you process that?

You've got a ton of data. What do you do?

Users send hundreds of messages per minute. Now what?

You could learn Elixir and Erlang – purpose built languages for message processing used in networking. But is that where you want your career to go?

You could try Kafka[120] or Hadoop[121]. Tools designed for big data, used by large organizations for mind-boggling amounts of data. Are you ready for that?

Elixir, Erlang, Kafka, Hadoop are wonderful tools, if you know how to use them. But there's a significant learning curve and devops work to keep them running.

You have to maintain servers, write code in obscure languages, and deal with problems we're trying to avoid.

120 https://kafka.apache.org/
121 https://hadoop.apache.org/

Serverless data processing

Instead, you can leverage existing skills to build a data processing pipeline.

I've used this approach to process millions of daily events with barely a 0.0007% loss of data. A rate of 7 events lost per 1,000,000.[122]

We used it to gather business and engineering analytics. A distributed `console.log` that writes to a central database. That's how I know you should never build a distributed logging system unless it's your core business 😓

The system accepts batches of events, adds info about user and server state, then saves each event for easy retrieval.

It was so convenient, we even used it for tracing and debugging in production. Pepper your code with `console.log`, wait for an error, see what happened.

---

122 Our dataloss happened because of Postgres. Sometimes it would fail to insert a row, but wouldn't throw an error. We mitigated with various workarounds but a small loss remained. At that point we decided it was good enough.

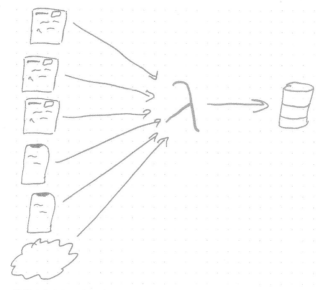

Figure 0.5: High level architecture for distributed logging and tracing

A similar system can process almost anything.

Great for problems you can split into independent tasks like prepping data. Less great for large inter-dependent operations like machine learning.

Architectures for serverless data processing

Serverless data processing works like .map and .reduce at scale. Inspired by Google's infamous MapReduce programming model[123] and used by big data processing frameworks.

Work happens in 3 steps:

1. Accept chunks of data
2. **Map** over your data
3. **Reduce** into output format

Say you're building an adder: multiply every number by 2 then sum.

Using functional programming patterns in JavaScript, you'd write code like this:

```
const result = [1, 2, 3, 4, 5] // input array
  .map(n => n * 2) // multiply each by 2
  .reduce((sum, n) => sum + n, 0) // sum together
```

Each step is independent.

123 https://en.wikipedia.org/wiki/MapReduce

The n => n*2 function only needs n. The (sum, n) => sum+n function needs the current sum and n.

That means you can distribute the work. Run each on a separate Lambda in parallel. Thousands at a time.

You go from a slow algorithm to as fast as a single operation, known as Amdahl's Law[124]. With infinite scale, you could process an array of 10,000,000 elements almost as fast as an array of 10.

Lambda limits you to 1000 parallel invocations. Individual steps can be slow (like when transcoding video) and you're limited by the reduce step.

Performance is best when reduce is un-necessary. Performance is worst when reduce needs to iterate over every element in 1 call and can't be distributed.

124 https://en.wikipedia.org/wiki/Amdahl%27s_law

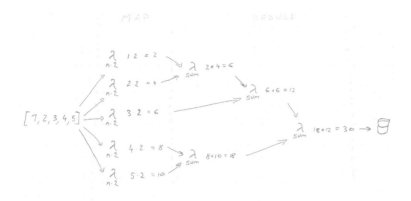

Figure 0.6: **Distributed adder architecture**

Our adder is commutative[125] and we can parallelize the reduce step using chunks of data.

In practice you'll find transformations that don't need a reduce step or require many maps. All follow this basic approach. :)

For the comp sci nerds ☞ this has no impact on big-O complexity[126] . You're changing real-world performance, not the algorithm.

125 https://en.wikipedia.org/wiki/Commutative_property
126 https://en.wikipedia.org/wiki/Big_O_notation

Build a distributed data processing pipeline

Let's build that adder and learn how to construct a robust massively distributed data processing pipeline. We're keeping the operation simple so we can focus on the architecture.

Here's the JavaScript code we're distributing:

```javascript
const result = [1, 2, 3, 4, 5] // input array
  .map((n) => n * 2) // multiply each by 2
  .reduce((sum, n) => sum + n, 0) // sum together
```

Following principles from the Architecture Principles[127] chapter, we're building a system that is:

- easy to understand
- robust against errors
- debuggable
- replayable
- always inspectable

We're going to use 3 Serverless Elements[128] to get there:

127 /serverless-architecture-principles
128 /serverless-elements

1. lambdas
2. queues
3. storage

You can see the full code on GitHub[129] .

The elements

We're using 3 lambdas, 2 queues, and 2 DynamoDB tables.

3 Lambdas

1. `sumArray` is our API-facing lambda. Accepts a request and kicks off the process
2. `timesTwo` is the map lambda. Accepts a number, multiplies by 2, and triggers the next step.
3. `reduce` combines intermediary steps into the final result. It's the most complex.

Our lambdas are written in TypeScript and each does 1 part of the process.

2 Queues

1. `TimesTwoQueue` holds messages from `sumArray` and calls `timesTwo`.

129   https://github.com/Swizec/serverlesshandbook.dev/tree/master/
examples/serverless-data-pipeline-example

2. ReduceQueue holds messages from `timesTwo` and calls reduce, which also uses the queue to trigger itself.

We're using SQS – Simple Queue Service – queues[130] for their reliability. An SQS queue stores messages for up to 14 days and keeps retrying until your Lambda succeeds.

When something goes wrong there's little chance a message gets lost unless you're eating errors. If your code doesn't throw, SQS interprets that as success.

You can configure max retries and how long a message should stick around. When it exceeds those deadlines, you can configure a Dead Letter Queue to store the message.

DLQ's are useful for processing bad messages. Send an alert to yourself, store it in a different table, debug what's going on.

2 tables

1. `scratchpad table` for intermediary results from `timesTwo`. This table makes reduce easier to implement and debug.
2. `sums table` for final results

---

130 https://aws.amazon.com/sqs/

Step 1 – the API

You first need to get data into the system. We use a Serverless
REST API[131].

```
# serverless.yml
functions:
  sumArray:
    handler: dist/sumArray.handler
    events:
      - http:
          path: sumArray
          method: POST
          cors: true
    environment:
      timesTwoQueueURL:
        Ref: TimesTwoQueue
```

sumArray is an endpoint that accepts POST requests and pipes
them into the sumArray.handler function. We set the URL for
our TimesTwoQueue as an environment variable.

Define the queue like this:

---

131 /serverless-rest-api

```
# serverless.yml
resources:
  Resources:
    TimesTwoQueue:
      Type: "AWS::SQS::Queue"
      Properties:
        QueueName: "TimesTwoQueue-\

↪  ${self:provider.stage}"
        VisibilityTimeout: 60
```

It's an SQS queue postfixed with the current stage, which helps us split between production and development.

The VisibilityTimeout[132] says that when your Lambda accepts a message, it has 60 seconds to process. After that, SQS assumes you never received the message and tries again.

Distributed systems are fun like that.

The sumArray.ts Lambda that accepts requests looks like this:

132   https://docs.aws.amazon.com/AWSSimpleQueueService/latest/
SQSDeveloperGuide/sqs-visibility-timeout.html

```typescript
// src/sumArray.ts

export const handler = async (event: APIGatewayEvent):
↪   Promise<APIResponse> => {
  const arrayId = uuidv4()

  if (!event.body) {
    return response(400, {
      status: "error",
      error: "Provide a JSON body",
    })
  }

  const array: number[] = JSON.parse(event.body)

  // split array into elements
  // trigger timesTwo lambda for each entry
  for (let packetValue of array) {
    await sendSQSMessage(process.env.timesTwoQueueURL!, {
      arrayId,
      packetId: uuidv4(),
      packetValue,
      arrayLength: array.length,
      packetContains: 1,
    })
  }

  return response(200, {
    status: "success",
    array,
```

```
        arrayId,
    })
}
```

Get API request, create an `arrayId`, parse JSON body, iterate over the input, return success and the new `arrayId`. Consumers can later use this ID identify their result.

Triggering the next step

We turn each element of the input array into a processing packet and send it to our SQS queue as a message.

```
// src/timesTwo.ts

for (let packetValue of array) {
  await sendSQSMessage(process.env.timesTwoQueueURL!, {
    arrayId,
    packetId: uuidv4(),
    packetValue,
    arrayLength: array.length,
    packetContains: 1,
```

```
  })
}
```

Each packet contains:

- `arrayId` to identify which input it belongs to
- `packetId` to identify the packet itself
- `packetValue` as the value. You could use this to store entire JSON blobs.
- `arrayLength` to help reduce know how many packets to expect
- `packetContains` to help reduce know when it's done

Most properties are metadata to help our pipeline. `packetValue` is the data we're processing.

`sendSQSMessage`[133] is a helper method that sends an SQS message using the AWS SDK.

Step 2 – the map

Our map uses the `timesTwo` lambda and handles each packet in isolation.

---

133   https://github.com/Swizec/serverlesshandbook.dev/blob/master/
examples/serverless-data-pipeline-example/src/utils.ts#L11

```yaml
# serverless.yml
functions:
  timesTwo:
    handler: dist/timesTwo.handler
    events:
      - sqs:
          arn:
            Fn::GetAtt:
              - TimesTwoQueue
              - Arn
          batchSize: 1
    environment:
      reduceQueueURL:
        Ref: ReduceQueue
```

timesTwo handles events from the TimesTwoQueue using the
timesTwo.handler method. It gets the reduceQueueURL as an
environment variable to trigger the next step.

AWS and SQS call our lambda and keep retrying when something
goes wrong. Perfect to let you re-deploy when there's a bug ✌️

The lambda looks like this:

```
// src/sumArray.ts

export const handler = async (event: SQSEvent) => {
  // grab messages from queue
  // depending on batchSize there could be multiple
  let packets: Packet[] = event.Records.map((record:
↪   SQSRecord) =>
    JSON.parse(record.body)
  )

  // iterate packets and multiply by 2
  // this would be a more expensive operation usually
  packets = packets.map((packet) => ({
    ...packet,
    packetValue: packet.packetValue * 2,
  }))

  // store each result in scratchpad table
  // in theory it's enough to put them on the queue
  // an intermediary table makes the reduce step
  // easier to implement
  await Promise.all(
    packets.map((packet) =>
      db.updateItem({
        TableName: process.env.SCRATCHPAD_TABLE!,
        Key: { arrayId: packet.arrayId, packetId:
↪   packet.packetId },
        UpdateExpression:
          "SET packetValue = :packetValue, \
          arrayLength = :arrayLength, \
```

```
        packetContains = :packetContains",
      ExpressionAttributeValues: {
        ":packetValue": packet.packetValue,
        ":arrayLength": packet.arrayLength,
        ":packetContains": packet.packetContains,
      },
    })
  )
)

// trigger next step in calculation
const uniqueArrayIds = Array.from(
  new Set(packets.map((packet) => packet.arrayId))
)

await Promise.all(
  uniqueArrayIds.map((arrayId) =>
    sendSQSMessage(process.env.reduceQueueURL!, \
              arrayId)
  )
)

  return true
}
```

Accept an event from SQS, parse JSON body, do the work, store intermediary results, trigger reduce step for each input.

SQS might call your lambda with multiple messages depending on your batchSize config. This helps you optimize cost and find the right balance between the number of executions and execution time.

Trigger the next step

Triggering the next step happens in 2 parts

1. store intermediary result
2. trigger next lambda

Storing intermediary results makes implementing the next lambda easier. We're building a faux queue on top of DynamoDB. That's okay because it makes the system easier to debug.

Something went wrong? Check intermediary table, see what's up.

We iterate over results, fire a DynamoDB updateItem query, and await the queries.

```
// src/timesTwo.ts

// store each result in scratchpad table
// in theory it's enough to put them on the queue
// an intermediary table makes the reduce step
// easier to implement
await Promise.all(
```

```
packets.map((packet) =>
  db.updateItem({
    TableName: process.env.SCRATCHPAD_TABLE!,
    Key: { arrayId: packet.arrayId, packetId:
↪  packet.packetId },
    UpdateExpression:
      "SET packetValue = :packetValue, arrayLength =
↪    :arrayLength, packetContains =
↪    :packetContains",
    ExpressionAttributeValues: {
      ":packetValue": packet.packetValue,
      ":arrayLength": packet.arrayLength,
      ":packetContains": packet.packetContains,
    },
  })
  )
)
```

Each entry in this table is uniquely identified with a combination of
arrayId and packetId.

Triggering the next step happens in another loop.

```
// src/timesTwo.ts

// trigger next step in calculation
const uniqueArrayIds = Array.from(
```

```
  new Set(packets.map((packet) => packet.arrayId))
)

await Promise.all(
  uniqueArrayIds.map((arrayId) =>
    sendSQSMessage(process.env.reduceQueueURL!, arrayId)
  )
)
```

We use an ES6 Set to get a list of unique array ids from our input message. You never know what gets jumbled up on the queue and you might receive multiple inputs in parallel.

Distributed systems are fun :)

For each unique input, we trigger a reduce lambda via ReduceQueue. A single reduce stream makes this example easier. You should aim for parallelism in production.

Step 3 – reduce

Combining intermediary steps into the final result is the most complex part of our example.

The simplest approach is to take the entire input and combine in 1 step. With large datasets this becomes impossible. Especially if combining elements is a big operation.

You could combine 2 elements at a time and run the reduce step in parallel.

Fine-tuning for number of invocations and speed of execution will result in an N somewhere between 2 and All. Optimal numbers depend on what you're doing.

Our reduce function uses the scratchpad table as a queue:

1. Take 2 elements
2. Combine
3. Write the new element
4. Delete the 2 originals

Like this:

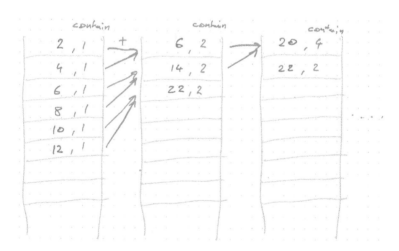

At each invocation we take 2 packets:

```
{
    arrayId: // ...
    packetId: // ...
    packetValue: 2,
    packetContains: 1,
    arrayLength: 10
}

{
    arrayId: // ...
    packetId: // ...
    packetValue: 4,
    packetContains: 1,
    arrayLength: 10
}
```

And combine them into a new packet

```
// +
{
    arrayId: // ...
    packetId: // ...
    packetValue: 6
    packetContains: 2,
    arrayLength: 10
}
```

When the count of included packets - packetContains - matches the total array length - arrayLength - we know this is the final result and write it into the results table.

Like I said, this is the complicated part.

The reduce step code

In code, the reduce step starts like any other lambda:

```
// src/reduce.ts
export const handler = async (event: SQSEvent) => {
  // grab messages from queue
  // depending on batchSize there could be multiple
  let arrayIds: string[] = event.Records.map((record:
  ↪  SQSRecord) =>
    JSON.parse(record.body)
  )

  // process each ID from batch
  await Promise.all(arrayIds.map(reduceArray))
}
```

Grab arrayIds from the SQS event and wait until every reduceArray call is done.

Then the reduceArray function does its job:

```
// src/reduce.ts

async function reduceArray(arrayId: string) {
  // grab 2 entries from scratchpad table
  // IRL you'd grab as many as you can cost-effectively
  ↪  process in execution
  // depends what you're doing
  const packets = await readPackets(arrayId)

  if (packets.length > 0) {
    // sum packets together
    const sum = packets.reduce(
      (sum: number, packet: Packet) => sum +
  ↪ packet.packetValue,
      0
    )

    // add the new item sum to scratchpad table
    // we do this first so we
        // don't delete rows if it fails
    const newPacket = {
      arrayId,
      packetId: uuidv4(),
      arrayLength: packets[0].arrayLength,
      packetValue: sum,
      packetContains: packets.reduce(
        (count: number, packet: Packet) => count +
  ↪ packet.packetContains,
        0
      ),
```

```
  }
  await db.updateItem({
    TableName: process.env.SCRATCHPAD_TABLE!,
    Key: {
      arrayId,
      packetId: uuidv4(),
    },
    UpdateExpression:
      "SET packetValue = :packetValue, arrayLength =
      ↪  :arrayLength, packetContains =
      ↪  :packetContains",
    ExpressionAttributeValues: {
      ":packetValue": newPacket.packetValue,
      ":arrayLength": newPacket.arrayLength,
      ":packetContains": newPacket.packetContains,
    },
  })

  // delete the 2 rows we just summed
  await cleanup(packets)

  // are we done?
  if (newPacket.packetContains >= \
        newPacket.arrayLength) {
    // done, save sum to final table
    await db.updateItem({
      TableName: process.env.SUMS_TABLE!,
      Key: {
        arrayId,
      },
      UpdateExpression: "SET resultSum = :resultSum",
      ExpressionAttributeValues: {
```

```
            ":resultSum": sum,
        },
    })
} else {
    // not done, trigger another reduce step
    await sendSQSMessage(process.env.reduceQueueURL!,
↪   arrayId)
    }
  }
}
```

Gets 2 entries from the DynamoDB table[134] and combines them into a new packet.

This packet *must* have a new packetId. It's a new entry for the faux processing queue on DynamoDB.

Insert that back. If it succeeds, remove the previous 2 elements using their arrayId/packetId combination.

If our new packetContains is greater than or equal to the total arrayLength, we know the computation is complete. Write results to the final table.

---

134 We use a Limit: 2 argument to limit how much of the table we scan through. Don't need more than 2, don't read more than 2. Keeps everything snappy

Conclusion

Lambda processing pipelines are a powerful tool that can process large amounts of data in near real-time. I have yet to find a way to swamp one of these in production.

Slow downs happen where you have to introduce throttling to limit processing because a downstream system can't take the load.

Next chapter, we talk about monitoring serverless apps.

Monitoring serverless apps

When clients have a bug, you can tell. Go through the flow, click around, see what happens.

But code on the server is invisible. And always broken[135] . A distributed system is never 100% error-free.

A good architecture[136] lets you ignore many errors. The system recovers on its own.

What about the bad errors? And how do you debug code you can't see?

Observability

Observability is the art of understanding the internal state of a system based on its outputs. It's a continuous process.

A good system lets you:

- understand what's going on
- see trends
- figure out what happened after an error
- *predict* errors
- know when there's an emergency
- understand how to fix an emergency

135 /robust-backend-design
136 /serverless-architecture-principles

Those are design goals. There is no right answer. Observability is an art and getting it right takes practice.

But there are guidelines you can follow. You'll need:

- **logs** are immutable events that happened in your system. They follow a structured format and offer information about what happened where and when.
- **metrics** are aggregate events over time. They tell you how much of what is happening, how long it takes, and help you understand trends.
- **traces** are journeys through the system. A sequence of events that contributed to a bigger result.

Questions to ask yourself

Observability is part of your development process. You can't tack it on later.

I like to ask these questions when building:

1. How will you know this works?
2. How will you know this broke?
3. How will you deduce where it broke?
4. How will you figure out how it broke?
5. How will you know which payload broke it?

There is no right answer. It takes a few emergencies to dial it in and save the info you need.

When do you need observability?

Always. ☺

It depends. How critical is your software?

When you have 10 users, eh I'd focus on getting users. When you have 100 users, eh they'll tell you when there's a bug.

You'll see stranger and stranger bugs the more users you have. A 1-in-1000 bug happens every day when you have 1000 users. At Google scale, tiny impossible-to-reproduce bugs happen every minute.

That's when observability shines. Understanding bugs you can't reproduce.

PS: you don't need traditional "monitoring" in a serverless system. Your server is never down, your memory is never full, your storage never runs out, your CPU is never busy.

What to measure

Deciding what to measure is a art. You'll get it wrong.

You build a system asking the 5 questions we mentioned. Add a bunch of measurements and walk away.

A few days pass and something goes wrong.

You go through the logs. There's too many. You ignore 80%.

You realize the 20% that are useful don't have enough info. Despite your best efforts, you can't be certain what happened.

Adjust what you log, add the info you wish you had, remove the info you didn't need. Next time will be better.

It's an iterative process :)

Typical useful logs and events

You need two types of logs:

1. The system is ticking along
2. Errors

Happy logs work like breadcrumbs.

You leave them behind so you can later trace a path through the system. How did this user get into that state? Are we seeing bottlenecks? Did event B that always comes after event A suddenly stop coming?

You want to know when a typical behavior changes.

Errors - always log errors. Add as much debugging info as possible. Print the whole stack trace, the exact error, and any identifiers you'll need to reproduce the bug.

Metrics to track

Specific metrics depend on what you care about.

Got a function that needs to be fast? Measure its speed. Got a suspected bottleneck? Measure requests waiting. Got a flaky process? Measure error rate.

At the least, you'll want to measure 3 metrics for each part of your system:

1. **Throughput** – how many requests are you processing
2. **Error rate** – how many errors happen
3. **Failure rate** – how many requests never succeed

"Part of the system" means an end-to-end process as seen by a user. Don't sweat individual pieces unless you identify a problem that needs a closer look.

When to alarm

Metrics help when you look at them, logs help when you're solving a problem. Alarms come to you.

An escalating system works best:

- email for small problems
- slack when the fire grows

- SMS for critical issues

You'll want to set alarms for high error and failure rates (depends what you consider high) and anomalies in throughput. When a 100/hour event drops to zero, something's wrong.

How to set alarms depends on your tool of choice. On AWS, Cloud-Watch offers basic support and I've loved DataDog in the past. Anomaly detection on DataDog is wonderful. 👍

Distributed logging

Logging is the core of your observability toolbox. Metrics and traces build on top of logs.

In a serverless system, you can't sign into a server to see the logs. There's no server and your system is distributed across many services.

You'll need a distributed logging system.

On AWS, you can achieve this through CloudWatch. A service that collects output from your lambdas and offers a basic UI.

StatsD

When you outgrow default CloudWatch metrics and need deeper insights, there's a rich ecosystem of tools and resources waiting for you. All built on top of a de facto standard: StatsD[137].

StatsD is an open source agent that listens for prints in a specific format to collect as metrics. It sends those to a central location without interfering with your code.

You can use StatsD with CloudWatch[138] to collect custom metrics. These show up in the CloudWatch UI.

Print logs like this:

```
console.log(
  "MetricName:value|type|sample_rate|tag1,tag2"
)
```

Sample rate and tags are optional.

When you print in that format, you can connect a number of 3rd party tools that give you power beyond the CloudWatch UI. Data-Dog[139] has been a great choice for me.

137 https://github.com/statsd/statsd
138   https://docs.aws.amazon.com/AmazonCloudWatch/latest/monitoring/
CloudWatch-Agent-custom-metrics-statsd.html
139 https://www.datadoghq.com

Make a pulse dashboard

The final step in your observability journey is a nice dashboard. Something you can look at, see wiggly lines, and say *"Yep, system's working"*

Dashboard your critical metrics. What you're focusing on *right now*. 5 or 6 at most.

You can build detailed dashboards for specific parts of your system. That comes when your project grows.

A typical core dashboard includes:

- global request throughput
- global error rate
- global failure rate
- response times

And remember: A metric that isn't actionable is pure vanity and should be removed.

Next chapter we look at the split between localhost and production.

Serverless dev, QA, and prod

You're building an app and want to show a friend. Do you ship to production?

You're trying a new feature that doesn't do localhost. Do you publish?

You've built a pipeline that edits user data and want to make sure it works. Test in production?

If you're brave enough ...

Before there's users

None of this matters until you have users. Build on the main branch, ship to production, test in real life. Enjoy yourself!

Coding at this stage is *fun*.

You don't have to worry about corrupting user data. No concerns about disrupting a user's workflow. You don't even need to worry about shipping bugs!

If nobody noticed the bug, was the bug even there?

A word of caution: It's easy to fill your database with crappy data. Try to start production clean.

Thank me later when counting users isn't a 5 step process. You'd be surprised how hard it can be to answer *"How many users do we have?"*.

Localhost vs. Production

Once you have users, you need a way to distinguish production from development. That's easy on a solo project.

Localhost is for development, production is for production. Run a copy of production on your machine and test.

The bigger your system, the trickier this gets. You need to host a database, run queues, caching layers, etc.

You can get close with the LocalStack plugin for the Serverless Framework[140] . But only production is like production. ✌

Plus you can't show off localhost to a friend or coworker.

The 3 stage split

A common solution to the production vs. development problem is the 3 stage split:

0. localhost
1. development
2. staging / QA
3. production

You build and test on localhost. Get fast iteration and reasonable certainty that your code works.

140 https://www.serverless.com/plugins/serverless-localstack

With the Serverless Framework, you can run lambdas locally[141] like this:

```
sls invoke local --function yourFunction
```

You then push to development. A deployed environment that's like production, but changes lots. Data is irrelevant, used by everyone on the team.

The development environment helps you test your code with others' work. You can show off to a friend, coworker, or product manager for early feedback.

When that works, you push to staging. A more stable environment used to test code right before it ships. Features are production ready, early feedback incorporated.

Staging is the playground for QA and final sign-off from product managers.

Then you push to production. 🚀

How to use the 3 stage split

Infrastructure-as-code makes the 3 stage split easy to set up. Have 3 branches of your codebase, deploy each to its own stage.

141   https://www.serverless.com/framework/docs/providers/aws/cli-reference/invoke-local/

With the serverless framework, you configure the deploy stage in
`serverless.yml`:

```
# serverless.yml
service: my-service

provider:
    name: aws
    stage: dev
```

Deploy with `sls deploy` and that creates or updates the `dev`
stage.

Stages work via name-spacing. Every resource embeds the stage
as part of its name and URL. Keep that in mind when naming resources manually.

Like when naming a queue:

```
# serverless.yml
resources:
  Resources:
    TimesTwoQueue:
```

```
Type: "AWS::SQS::Queue"
Properties:
  # include the stage variable in your name
  QueueName: "TimesTwoQueue-\
              ${self:provider.stage}"
```

Current stage is embedded in the string through the
${self:provider.stage} variable.

Dynamic stages

Editing the stage in serverless.yml on every deploy is annoying.
Pass it in the command line instead.

```
# serverless.yml

provider:
    name: aws
    # use stage option, dev by default
    stage: ${opt:stage, "dev"}
```

Deploy with sls deploy --stage prod to deploy to
production. Defaults to dev.

Use a new stage to set up a new environment, existing stage to update. The framework figures it out for you.

Make sure stage names match your .env.X configuration files[142] .

Deploy previews

The 3 stage split starts breaking down around the 6 to 7 engineers mark. More if your projects are small, less if they're big.

You start stepping on each other's toes.

Alice is working on a big feature and she'll need 3 months. During that time none of her work can go to production. She'd like to test on development.

Bob meanwhile is fixing bugs and keeping the lights on. He needs to merge his work into development, staging, and production every day.

How can Bob and Alice work together?

There's 2 solutions:

1. Deploy previews
2. Feature flags

142 /handling-secrets

With infrastructure-as-code, deploy previews are the simple solution. Create a new stage for every large feature, deploy, show off, and test.

You get an isolated environment with all the working bits and pieces. Automate it with GitHub Actions to create a new stage for every pull request.

That's the model Netlify and Vercel champion. Every pull request is automatically deployed on a new copy of production with every update. 👍

Trunk-based development

A popular approach in large teams is trunk-based development.

Everyone works on the main branch, deploys to production regularly, and uses feature flags to disable features before they're ready. A strong automated testing culture is critical.

Google uses the Beyonce rule[143] :

> If you liked it, you shoulda put a test on it

Anyone can change any code at any time. Tests help you prevent accidents.

143   https://www.oreilly.com/library/view/software-engineering-at/ 9781492082781/ch01.html

Feature flags let you disable new features before they're ready. Your code hits production quickly which ensures it doesn't break. If you refactored something, others can use it. If you created new functionality, it's available.

But you disable user-facing parts of your feature to avoid a broken experience.

Implementing feature flags can be as easy as an environment variable with a bunch of IF statements, or as complex as progressive canary deploys. Those let you reveal a feature to 1% of users, then 5%, then 10, ...

Which approach should you pick?

The best approach depends on team size, established norms, correctness requirements, and your deployment environment.

If you have a clean infrastructure-as-code approach, creating new stages is great. If you need manual setup, the 3 stage approach is best.

You can even split your project into sub-projects. Isolated areas of concern that can move and deploy independently. Known as microservices.

And remember, the easier your code is to fix and deploy, the less you have to worry about any of this. **Optimize for fast iteration over avoiding mistakes.**

For side projects I like to test in production. Live wild 🤘

Next chapter, we look at how to think about serverless performance.

Serverless performance

Performance talks about what you get per unit of a resource. Time, effort, space, energy, and money.

How much of X does it take to get N results?

We've touched on performance before. Mentioned scaling strategies in Pros and Cons of Serverless[144] and Databases[145] , talked about complexity in Lambda Pipelines[146] , and mentioned flow in Robust Backend Design[147] .

But what do you measure? What's achievable? Where do you optimize? How does serverless stack up?

The performance trifecta

Software systems care about time, money, and space. You have to balance all 3.

With metered pricing, serverless lets you pay directly for execution time, memory size, and storage space. No overhead. You don't use it, you don't pay it.

AWS Lambda charges for execution time with millisecond precision[148] .

144 /serverless-pros-cons
145 /databases
146 /lambda-pipelines
147 /robust-backend-design
148 https://amzn.to/3sAh2qs

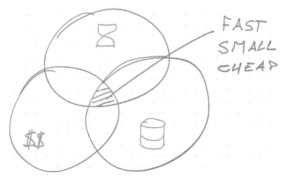

Figure 0.7: Fast, small, cheap

Faster code uses more memory to gain speed. Or you can beef up CPU. Both make your code more expensive to run.

Saving storage space costs CPU time to compress and clean data. Storage is cheap. Bandwidth to and from storage gets pricey.

You **optimize memory** with slower code. Memory is plentiful these days, but not in serverless. You want small functions.

Every optimization takes **human time and effort**. A metric that software *organizations* care about. How hard is the code to develop and maintain?

You can think of performance as a 4-dimensional optimization function. **Speed vs. space vs. money vs. effort**. Great question for a calculus exam.

Avoid doing the calculus with ye olde law of prioritization:

1. Make it work
2. Make it right
3. Make it fast

You'll find that computers are fast & cheap and humans are slow & expensive. Stick to 1, add 2 for easier maintenance. 3 when necessary.

Where size matters

Storage is cheap – \$0.023/GB/month on S3[149] – and memory is *pretty* cheap at \$0.000016/GB/second[150] . Memory cost per unit *increases* when you need extra. Storage cost per unit *decreases* when you use more.

149 https://aws.amazon.com/s3/pricing/
150 https://aws.amazon.com/lambda/pricing/

Bandwidth is where size gets you. AWS charges for taking data out of the system. Other providers are similar.

You pay to send data to users or between availability zones. Details depend on which services are involved. For example: S3 to CloudFront (the CDN) is free, then CloudFront charges $0.085/GB.

Minimize what you send over the wire.

Thinking about speed

2 metrics matter for "speed":

1. Latency
2. Throughput

Best summarized with a metaphor from Andrew S. Tanenbaum[151]

> Never underestimate the bandwidth of a station wagon full of tapes hurtling down the highway

151 https://en.wikipedia.org/wiki/Andrew_S._Tanenbaum

Latency

Latency measures delay. How long does it take to start working?

You can write the fastest code in the world, but if it takes 2 seconds to get started you'll have unhappy users.

The biggest factors are:

- network time
- internal routing
- lambda wake up time

Network time measures how long it takes for a user's request to reach your server. Depends on distance and connection quality.

Routing is internal to your serverless provider. How long does it take to accept a request and send it to your code? Security rules can make this slower or faster.

Lambda wake up time measures how long it takes to spin up your tiny server. Depends on bundle size, runtime environment, and how your code warms up.

Throughput

Throughput measures how fast you work. When you get a request, how long does it take?

The biggest factors are:

- code performance
- input/output

Serverless is for small distributed operations[152]. Code performance and algorithm complexity have little impact.

> Fancy algorithms are slow when N is small, and N is usually small. Fancy algorithms have big constants. Until you know that N is frequently going to be big, don't get fancy. Rob Pike[a]
>
> _____
>
> *a* https://en.wikipedia.org/wiki/Rob_Pike

That leaves **input/output**.

Waiting for a database, talking to 3rd party APIs, loading a web page, those will *destroy* your performance.

The average duration for my screenshot lambda is 10 seconds. Mostly waiting for Chrome to start and webpages to load.

You pay for every millisecond of that wait. 😊

_____

152 /lambda-pipelines

Thinking about scalability

Scalability[153] talks about how your system behaves as load grows.

What happens at 10 requests per day? What about 10,000,000?

Your system is considered scalable, if resources grow linearly or less with demand. Using 1 lambda per request may not be cheap, but it does scale.

A system that grows faster than demand blows up eventually.

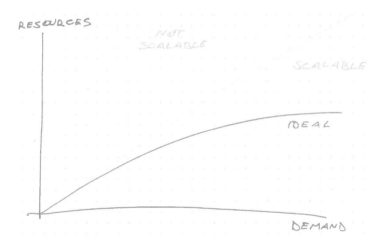

This applies to teams as much as it does to computers. If you need 3 new developers to do 2x more work, your company will die.

Scaling your software comes in 2 flavors: vertical and horizontal. Use a mix of both.

153 https://en.wikipedia.org/wiki/Scalability

Vertical scaling

Vertical scaling is the art of getting 1 computational resource to do more.

This type of scaling can get expensive. You need more resources – faster CPU, more memory, better hardware, a GPU – and lots of engineering effort to optimize your code.

For many workloads, this approach is best.

It's easier to scale a database by adding CPU and memory than by rebuilding your application to use more databases. AI researchers prefer a computer with terabytes of memory over tweaking algorithms to need less.

And sometimes it's the only way. Like processing a video.

Horizontal scaling

Horizontal scaling is the art of splitting work between computational resources.

This type of scaling can be cheap. Easier to provision, quicker to get going, less effort to optimize.

But you have to find a balance. 6 cheap computers can cost more than 3 expensive computers.

That's where serverless shines.

Horizontal scaling is perfect for isolated operations with little inter-dependency. Like API requests, processing a video library, or serving static files.

Use the map-reduce pattern[154] to split larger tasks like we did in the Lambda Pipelines chapter. You pay with system complexity.

Achieving speed

Never optimize your code until it tells you where it hurts. Bottlenecks are surprising and unpredictable. Measure.

But don't kick the table with your pinky toe either. You already know that hurts.

For maximum speed in serverless environments focus on:

- cold wake up times
- reducing input output
- fast simple code

Cold wake up times

Traditional servers split performance into warm and cold. The server starts cold and warms up its caches, algorithm setup, and execution environment with the first few requests.

154 /lambda-pipelines

Most requests reach a warm server which is orders of magnitude faster.

With serverless, every request could be cold.

There is no one solution I can give you. Optimizing cold boot performance takes work and understanding *your* software.

A few areas to look at:

- Use a language with a **fast and nimble runtime**. JavaScript is surprisingly effective, Go can work great. JVM-based languages tend to struggle.
- **Ruthlessly reduce bundle size**. The less code that needs to load, the better. Compile and minimize your source, remove un-needed dependencies[155] . Use the `exclude` config in `serverless.yml`.

155   https://www.serverless.com/framework/docs/providers/aws/guide/packaging#package-configuration

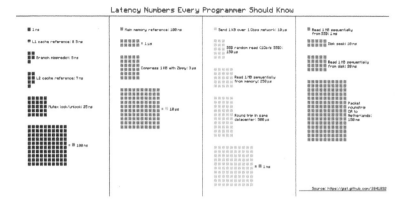

Figure 0.8: Latency numbers every programmer should know

- **Avoid fancy algorithms** with large constants. Iterating your data 5x to set up a fast algorithm may not be worth it. You're processing small payloads.

Reduce input output

The biggest performance killer is input/output. Your tiny server comes with no batteries included.

Want to read from cache? Network request. Database? Network request. Call an API? Yep, network.

Networks are slow[156] . If reading a variable is like brushing your teeth, a roundtrip with your database is like a 6 day vacation. 🐢

156 https://gist.github.com/hellerbarde/2843375

Providers optimize these "external" requests but you have no control and there are hard limits at play.

Best you can do is minimize.

- do more in 1 request (like bigger SQL queries)
- avoid I/O in a loop, try to pre-fetch
- prefer local memoization[157] over cache

Memoization vs. cache

Memoization stores results in a local variable. Call your function with the same inputs and return the value without recalculating.

But you lose memory when your lambda goes to bed. That's where a cache can help. A service with persistent memory that stores pre-computed values.

Like your database, the caching service is an external request. Much slower than a local variable.

Use memoization when you call the same code multiple times per request. Use cache when you need the same data across many requests.

When you get requests frequently enough, serverless providers reuse your code between executions. Memoizing in "global" memory does wonders.

157 https://en.wikipedia.org/wiki/Memoization

In pseudo-javascript:

```
let memoized = null

exports.handler = function (argument) {
  if (!memoized) {
    memoized = expensiveComputation()
  }

  return memoized
}
```

Fast simple code

Keep it simple.

Use the fastest check as your first argument in an && or || chain. Computers skip arguments that can't change the result.

Avoid doing work that you'll throw away 10 lines later.

An O(n) search can be faster than building a hashmap in O(n) and reading it once.

Think of your system as a whole

Once you've optimized individual components, it's time to look at your system as a whole. Find the bottlenecks.

> The fastest algorithm in the world is worthless
> when throttled by a slow database.

A bottleneck happens when there's a performance mismatch between parts of your system. Fast code feeding into slow code. Slow code that your whole system relies on ...

Typical offenders include:

- large computation (like video and image processing)
- poorly optimized databases
- 3rd party APIs

You can find the bottleneck by looking at your queues. Is one of them filling up with data? Likely feeding a bottleneck.

You can look at Lambda execution times. A slow Lambda could be full of bad code, more likely it's talking to a bottleneck.

Can you move it off the critical path[158] ? Cache or memoize any API and database responses?

158 https://en.wikipedia.org/wiki/Critical_path_method

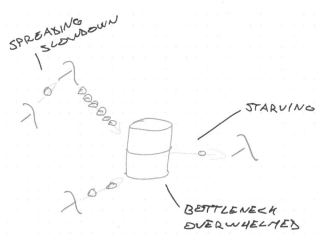

Figure 0.9: **Bottlenecks impact your whole system**

The exact answer depends on *your* code and *your* system.

Optimizing cost

> Value your time.

I talked to an AWS billing expert and that was the take-away. Then I killed the whole chapter on cost.

Your time is worth more than your bill.

However, he suggested you try AWS Lambda Power Tuning[159] . A tool that tries your lambda in different configurations and shows the balance between power, speed, and cost.

159 https://github.com/alexcasalboni/aws-lambda-power-tuning

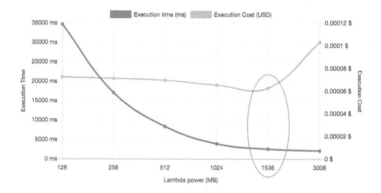

Figure 0.10: Example graph from AWS Lambda Power Tuning

Execution time goes from 35s with 128MB to less than 3s with 1.5GB, while being 14% cheaper to run.

A great example of how vertical scaling beats horizontal. But you keep every benefit of horizontal, because serverless. 🚀

Next chapter we look at running Serverless Chrome, a typical case where beefy lambdas help lots.

Serverless Chrome puppeteer

Say you want to build a scraper, automate manual testing, or generate custom social cards for your website. What do you do?

You could spin up a docker container, set up headless Chrome, add Puppeteer, write a script to run it all, add a server to create an API, and ...

Or you can set up Serverless Chrome with AWS Lambda. Write a bit of code, hit deploy, and get a Chrome browser running on demand.

That's what this chapter is about 🦾

You'll learn how to:

- configure Chrome Puppeteer on AWS
- build a basic scraper
- take website screenshots
- run it on-demand

We build a scraper that goes to google.com[160] , types in a phrase, and returns the first page of results. Then reuse the same code to return a screenshot.

You can see full code on GitHub[161]

---

160 https://google.com
161   https://github.com/Swizec/serverlesshandbook.dev/tree/master/
examples/serverless-chrome-example

Serverless Chrome

Chrome's engine ships as the open source Chromium browser. Other browsers use it and add their own UI and custom features.

You can use the engine for browser automation – scraping, testing, screenshots, etc. When you need to render a website, Chromium is your friend.

This means:

- download a chrome binary
- set up an environment that makes it happy
- run in headless mode
- configure processes that talk to each other via complex sockets

Others have solved this problem for you.

Rather than figure it out yourself, I recommend using chrome-aws-lambda[162] . It's the most up-to-date package for running Serverless Chrome.

162 https://github.com/alixaxel/chrome-aws-lambda

Here's what you need for a Serverless Chrome setup:

1. Install dependencies

```
$ yarn add chrome-aws-lambda@3.1.1 \
puppeteer@3.1.0 \
@types/puppeteer \
puppeteer-core@3.1.0
```

This installs everything you need to both run and interact with Chrome. ✌️

Check chrome-aws-lambda/README[163] for the latest version of Chrome Puppeteer you can use. Make sure they match.

2. configure serverless.yml

```
# serverless.yml

service: serverless-chrome-example

provider:
  name: aws
  runtime: nodejs12.x
  stage: dev
```

163 https://github.com/alixaxel/chrome-aws-lambda#versioning

```
package:
  exclude:
    - node_modules/puppeteer/.local-chromium/**
```

Configure a new service, make it run on AWS, use latest node.

The package part is important. It tells Serverless *not* to package the chromium binary with your code. AWS rejects builds of that size.

You are now ready to start running Chrome ✌️

Chrome Puppeteer 101

Chrome Puppeteer[164] is a set of tools to interact with Chrome programmatically.

> Puppeteer is a Node library which provides a
> high-level API to control Chrome or Chromium
> over the DevTools Protocol. Puppeteer runs
> headless by default, but can be configured to
> run full (non-headless) Chrome or Chromium.

164 https://pptr.dev/

Write code that interacts with a website like a person would. Anything a person can do on the web, you can do with Puppeteer.

Core syntax feels like jQuery, but the objects are different than what you're used to. I've found it's best not to worry about the details.

Here's how you click on a link:

```javascript
const page = await browser.newPage() // open a "tab"
page.goto("https://example.com") // navigates to URL

// grab a div
const div = await page.$("div#some_content")
await div.click("a.target_link") // clicks link
```

Always open a new page for every new browser context.

Navigate to your URL then use jQuery-like selectors to interact with the page. You can feed selectors into click() and other methods, or use the page.$ syntax to search around.

Build a scraper

Web scraping is fiddly but sounds simple in theory:

- load website
- find content
- read content
- return content in new format

But that doesn't generalize. Each website is different.

You adapt the core technique to each website you scrape and there's no telling when the HTML might change.

You might even find websites that actively fight against scraping. Block bots, limit access speed, obfuscate HTML, ...

Please play nice and don't unleash thousands of parallel requests onto unsuspecting websites.

You can watch me work on this project on YouTube, if you prefer video:

https://www.youtube.com/watch?v=wRJTxahPli4

And you can try the final result here: https://4tydwq78d9. execute-api.us-east-1.amazonaws.com/dev/scraper

1. more dependencies

Start with the `serverless.yml` and dependencies from earlier (chrome-aws-lambda and puppeteer).

Add `aws-lambda`:

```
$ yarn add aws-lambda @types/aws-lambda
```

Installs the code you need to interact with the AWS Lambda environment.

2. add a scraper function

Define a new scraper function in serverless.yml

```
# serverless.yml

functions:
  scraper:
    handler: dist/scraper.handler
    memorysize: 2536
    timeout: 30
    events:
      - http:
          path: scraper
          method: GET
          cors: true
```

We're saying code lives in the handler method exported from
scraper. We ask for lots of memory and a long timeout. Chrome

is resource intensive and our code makes web requests, which might take a while.

All this fires from a GET request on /scraper.

3. getChrome()

The getChrome method instantiates a new browser context. I like to put this in a util file.

```
// src/util.ts

import chrome from "chrome-aws-lambda"

export async function getChrome() {
  let browser = null

  try {
    browser = await chrome.puppeteer.launch({
      args: chrome.args,
      defaultViewport: {
        width: 1920,
        height: 1080,
        isMobile: true,
        deviceScaleFactor: 2,
      },
      executablePath: await chrome.executablePath,
```

```
      headless: chrome.headless,
      ignoreHTTPSErrors: true,
    })
  } catch (err) {
    console.error("Error launching chrome")
    console.error(err)
  }

  return browser
}
```

We launch a Chrome Puppeteer instance with default config and specify our own screen size.

The isMobile setting tricks many websites into loading faster. The deviceScaleFactor: 2 helps create better screenshots. It's like using a retina screen.

Adding ignoreHTTPSErrors makes the process more robust.

If the browser fails to launch, we log debugging info.

4. a shared createHandler()

We're building 2 pieces of code that share a lot of logic – scraping and screenshots. Both need a browser, deal with errors, and parse URL queries.

We build a common `createHandler()` method that deals with boilerplate and calls the important function when ready.

```typescript
// src/util.ts

import { APIGatewayEvent } from "aws-lambda"
import { Browser } from "puppeteer"

// scraper and screenshot have the same basic handler
// they just call a different method to do things
export const createHandler = (
  workFunction: (browser: Browser, search: string) \
      => Promise<APIResponse>
) => async (event: APIGatewayEvent): \
    Promise<APIResponse> => {
  const search =
    event.queryStringParameters &&
↪   event.queryStringParameters.search

  if (!search) {
    return {
      statusCode: 400,
      body: "Please provide a ?search= parameter",
    }
  }

  const browser = await getChrome()
```

```
      if (!browser) {
        return {
          statusCode: 500,
          body: "Error launching Chrome",
        }
      }

      try {
        // call the function that does the real work
        const response = await workFunction(browser, search)

        return response
      } catch (err) {
        console.log(err)
        return {
          statusCode: 500,
          body: "Error scraping Google",
        }
      }
    }
```

We read the ?search= param, open a browser, and verify everything's set up.

Then we call the passed-in workFunction, which returns a
response. If that fails, we throw a 500 error.

5. scrapeGoogle()

We're ready to scrape Google search results.

```
async function scrapeGoogle(browser: Browser, search:
↪  string) {
  const page = await browser.newPage()
  await page.goto("https://google.com", {
    waitUntil: ["domcontentloaded", "networkidle2"],
  })

  // this part is specific to the page you're scraping
  await page.type("input[type=text]", search)

  const [response] = await Promise.all([
    page.waitForNavigation(),
    page.click("input[type=submit]"),
  ])

  if (!response.ok()) {
    throw "Couldn't get response"
  }

  await page.goto(response.url())

  // specific to the page you're scraping
  const searchResults = await page.\$\$(".rc")

  let links = await Promise.all(
```

```
    searchResults.map(async (result) => {
      return {
        url: await result.$eval("a",
                    (node) => node.getAttribute("href")),
        title: await result.$eval("h3",
                    (node) => node.innerHTML),
        description: await result.$eval("span.st",
                    (node) => node.innerHTML),
      }
    })
  )

  return {
    statusCode: 200,
    body: JSON.stringify(links),
  }
}

export const handler = createHandler(scrapeGoogle)
```

Lots going on here. Let's go piece by piece.

```
const page = await browser.newPage()
await page.goto("https://google.com", {
```

```
  waitUntil: ["domcontentloaded", "networkidle2"],
})
```

Open a new page, navigate to google.com, wait for everything to load. I recommend waiting for `networkidle2`, which means all asynchronous requests have finished.

Useful when dealing with complex webapps.

```
// this part is specific to the page you're scraping
await page.type("input[type=text]", search)

const [response] = await Promise.all([
  page.waitForNavigation(),
  page.click("input[type=submit]"),
])

if (!response.ok()) {
  throw "Couldn't get response"
}

await page.goto(response.url())
```

To scrape google, we type a search into the input field, then hit submit and wait for the page to load.

This part is different for every website.

```
// this part is specific to the page you're scraping
const searchResults = await page.\$\$(".rc")

let links = await Promise.all(
  searchResults.map(async (result) => {
    return {
      url: await result.$eval("a",
              (node) => node.getAttribute("href")),
      title: await result.$eval("h3",
              (node) => node.innerHTML),
      description: await result.$eval("span.st",
              (node) => node.innerHTML),
    }
  })
)

return {
  statusCode: 200,
  body: JSON.stringify(links),
}
```

When the results page loads, we:

- look for every .rc DOM element – best identifier of search
  results I could find

- iterate through results
- get the info we want from each

You can use the page.$eval trick to parse DOM nodes with the same API you'd use in a browser. Executes your method on the nodes it finds and returns the result.

6. hit deploy and try it out

You now have a bonafide web scraper. Wakes up on demand, runs chrome, turns Google search results into easy-to-use JSON.

https://twitter.com/Swizec/status/1282446868950085632

We left out project configuration boilerplate. You can find those details in other chapters or see example code on GitHub[165] .

Take screenshots

Taking screenshots is similar to scraping. Instead of parsing the page, you call .screenshot() and get an image.

Our example returns that image directly. You'll want to store on S3 and return a URL in a real project. Lambda isn't a great fit for large files.

165   https://github.com/Swizec/serverlesshandbook.dev/tree/master/examples/serverless-chrome-example

1. tell API Gateway to serve binary

First, we tell API Gateway that it's okay to serve binary data.

I don't recommend this in production unless you have a great reason. Like a dynamic image that changes every time.

```
# serverless.yml

provider:
  name: aws
  runtime: nodejs12.x
  stage: dev
  apiGateway:
    binaryMediaTypes:
      - "*/*"
```

You can limit binaryMediaTypes to specific types you intend to use. */* is easier.

2. add a new function

Next we define a new Lambda function

```
# serverless.yml

functions:
  screenshot:
    handler: dist/screenshot.handler
    memorysize: 2536
    timeout: 30
    events:
      - http:
          path: screenshot
          method: GET
          cors: true
```

Same as before, different name. Needs lots of memory and a long timeout.

3. screenshotGoogle()

We're using similar machinery as before.

```
// src/screenshot.ts

async function screenshotGoogle(\
```

```
    browser: Browser, search: string) {
  const page = await browser.newPage()
  await page.goto("https://google.com", {
    waitUntil: ["domcontentloaded", "networkidle2"],
  })

  // specific to the page you're screenshotting
  await page.type("input[type=text]", search)

  const [response] = await Promise.all([
    page.waitForNavigation(),
    page.click("input[type=submit]"),
  ])

  if (!response.ok()) {
    throw "Couldn't get response"
  }

  await page.goto(response.url())

  // this part is specific to the page you're
  ↪  screenshotting
  const element = await page.$("#main")

  if (!element) {
    throw "Couldn't find results div"
  }

  const boundingBox = await element.boundingBox()
  const imagePath = `/tmp/screenshot-${new
↪  Date().getTime()}.png`
```

```
if (!boundingBox) {
  throw "Couldn't measure size of results div"
}

await page.screenshot({
  path: imagePath,
  clip: boundingBox,
})

const data = fs.readFileSync(imagePath)\
    .toString("base64")

return {
  statusCode: 200,
  headers: {
    "Content-Type": "image/png",
  },
  body: data,
  isBase64Encoded: true,
}
}

export const handler = createHandler(screenshotGoogle)
```

Same code up to when we load the results page. Type a query, hit submit, wait for reload.

Then we do something different – measure the size of our results div.

```javascript
// specific to the page you're screenshotting
const element = await page.$("#main")

if (!element) {
  throw "Couldn't find results div"
}

const boundingBox = await element.boundingBox()
const imagePath = `/tmp/screenshot-${new
↪   Date().getTime()}.png`

if (!boundingBox) {
  throw "Couldn't measure size of results div"
}
```

We look for results and grab their boundingBox(). That tells us the x, y coordinates and the width, height size for a more focused screenshot.

We set up an imagePath in /tmp. We can write to a file on Lambda's hard drive, *but it will not stay there*. When our lambda turns off, the file is gone.

```
await page.screenshot({
  path: imagePath,
  clip: boundingBox,
})
```

Take a screenshot with page.screenshot(). Saves to a file.

```
const data = fs.readFileSync(imagePath)\
  .toString("base64")

return {
  statusCode: 200,
  headers: {
    "Content-Type": "image/png",
  },
  body: data,
  isBase64Encoded: true,
}
```

Read the file into a Base64-encoded string and return a response. It must contain a content type – image/png in our case – and tell API Gateway that it's Base64-encoded.

This is where you'd upload to S3 in production.

You can try mine here: https://4tydwq78d9.execute-api. us-east-1.amazonaws.com/dev/screenshot

Or go to serverlesshandbook.dev/claim for interactive features.

How to use this

The most common use cases for Chrome Puppeteer are:

1. Running automated tests
2. Scraping websites cheaply
3. Generating dynamic HTML-to-PNG images
4. Generating PDFs

3 and 4 are great because you can build a small website that renders a social card for your content and use this machinery to turn it into an image.

Same for PDFs – build dynamic website, print-to-PDF with Chrome. Easier than generating PDFs by hand.

Have fun 😊

Next chapter we look at handling secrets.

Handling Secrets

How do you send an SMS when users click a button?

You find a JavaScript library that talks to an SMS provider. Configure your API keys, call the library, user gets an SMS. Yay!

3 months later you wake up to a $5,000 bill. Someone looked at your JavaScript code, took the API keys, and ran a spam campaign.

WHOOPSIES...

Orchestrating 3rd party services is where cloud functions shine. The perfect environment for glue code.

Isolated code that does *one* thing with no cruft. Runs on-demand, consumes no resources when not in use, scales near infinitely. Perfection.

And it runs on a server where users can't see the code. There's no right-click inspect, no JavaScript files downloaded, no user environment at all.

What is a secret

A secret is any piece of information you can't share. Any key with access to a special resource. Passwords and API tokens, for example.

You can add semi-secret configuration variables. URLs for parts of your system, ports of a database server, kinda-hardcoded data, etc.

How secretive you have to be depends on context.

Configuration variables are okay to leak, if the system is otherwise secure. But they can give an attacker information about your system.

Production passwords for sensitive health information ... you don't even want your engineers to know those. Especially not former engineers.

3 ways to handle secrets

There are 3 ways to handle secrets. From least to most secure.

1. Hardcoded values
2. Dotenv files
3. Secrets manager

Each method comes with different pros and cons. Pros in terms of security, cons in how cumbersome to use.

Hardcoded values in code

```
MY_SECRET_KEY="f3q20-98facv87432q4"
```

Hardcoded secrets are the easiest to use and the least secure.

They're okay for prototyping. Reduce moving pieces and focus on the API integration. Ignore the yak shaving around your goal.

Code runs on the server and users won't be able to steal your secrets.

But anyone with access to your code can see the secrets.

Share on GitHub and that includes the whole world. Bots always scrape GitHub looking for strings that look like keys. Your secret *will* be stolen.

AWS is paranoid enough that their own bot looks for secret keys. If they find yours, your AWS account gets locked. Ask me how I know[166] 😅

166 https://bit.ly/3fnzeQk

Another issue with hardcoded keys is that they're hard to change. You have to re-deploy every time. And you're forced to use the same account for testing and production.

Dotenv files

A step up from hardcoded keys are dotenv files – .env. Configuration files in your codebase that hold secrets.

```
# .env
MY_SECRET_KEY=f3q20-98facv87432q4
MY_API_URL=https://example.com
```

A .env file holds your secrets and configuration variables in one place. Makes them easier to use and change without searching through code.

You should *not* store these in version control. That's where the increased security comes from.

The common approach is to:

1. Have a blank .env file with every variable stored in version control

2. Every engineer makes a copy
3. Fills out values from team members or a shared passwords manager

You'll never leak secrets to GitHub by accident. But they're unencrypted on everyone's laptop, difficult to change across a large team, and packaged into your deploys.

Anyone who breaks into your laptop or steals a deploy package from S3 can read the secrets.

On the bright side, dotenv files are easy to split between environments. You can have `.env.local`, `.env.production`, `.env.development` with different values for every secret. ✌

How to use .env files

Many frameworks support `.env` files by default. Populate the file and read values from `process.env`.

When using the Serverless Framework, you'll need a plugin: `serverless-dotenv-plugin`. Here's what you do.

Install the plugin:

```
yarn add serverless-dotenv-plugin
```

Enable it in your serverless.yml config:

```
# serverless.yml
plugins:
  - serverless-dotenv-plugin
```

Run deploy and access values with process.env 🤘

You can match environment specific files to deployments using the stage: X config. serverless-dotenv-plugin reads the .env.X file that matches your stage.

Secrets manager

The most secure way to handle secrets is using a secrets manager.

A secrets manager works like the password manager in your browser. You have to authenticate to get access, re-authenticate every time, and secrets are encrypted when not in use.

You can even make your secrets double blind. *Nobody* needs to know their values.

Engineers can't see secrets in the code, they're not saved on anyone's laptop, you can't steal them from the server, and with the right configuration, secrets change every N days.

How to use a secrets manager

If you're on Netlify or Vercel, their secrets system is a secrets manager. They control the run-time and inject those values into `process.env`.

On AWS, you'll have to partially build your own.

First, save your secrets in AWS Secrets Manager[167] . Follow the wizard, it's great.

You can store many secret values in 1 configuration. I recommend grouping by environment – dev, staging, production – or use a logical grouping based on what you're doing. One secret per API.

Second, give your code permission to access secrets.

---

167 https://console.aws.amazon.com/secretsmanager/home

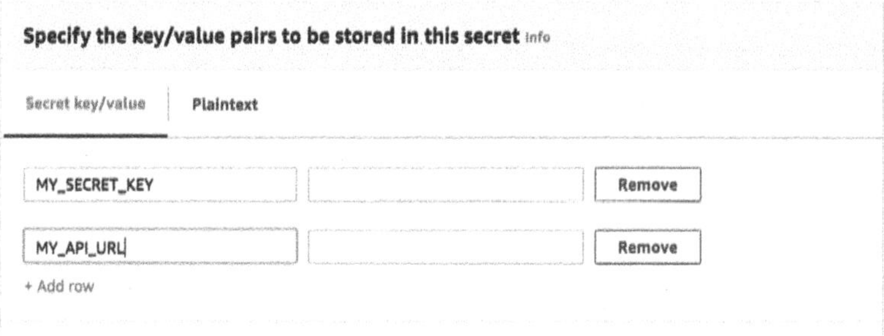

Specify the key/value pairs to be stored in this secret Info

Secret key/value   Plaintext

| MY_SECRET_KEY | | Remove |
| MY_API_URL | | Remove |

+ Add row

Figure 0.11: AWS Secrets Manager configuration

```
# serverless.yml
provider:
  # ...
  iamRoleStatements:
    - Effect: "Allow"
      Action:
        - "secretsmanager:GetSecretValue"
      Resource:
↪     "arn:aws:secretsmanager:${self:provider.region}:*"
```

You're giving permission to GetSecretValue, not to make changes. This is important. You do not want somebody hacking into your system and locking you out.

Using an asterisk – * – for secret name is convenient. For more security, limit access to specific secrets.

Third, access your secrets at runtime.

```
import { SecretsManager } from "aws-sdk"

const ssm = new SecretsManager({
  region: "us-east-1", // make sure this matches your
↪   region
})

const secret = await ssm
  .getSecretValue({ SecretId: "<your secret name>" })
  .promise()

const { MY_SECRET_KEY, MY_API_URL } =
↪   JSON.parse(secret?.SecretString)
```

This instantiates a new SSM client, gets your secret value, returns a JSON. Parse JSON, get secrets.

This is an API call that might fail[168] . Make sure to handle errors and fail correctly, if you can't get the secret.

You'll have to do this every time.

Fetching a fresh secret every time ensures that:

168 https://serverlesshandbook.dev/robust-backend-design

1. you get the latest value
2. you don't keep decrypted secrets in memory for long

However, this increases latency. You're making an API call that takes time. Not a lot, but not zero.

You can memoize secrets values in Lambda memory. Rely on the ephemeral nature of your environment to forget.

Conclusion

Choose the strategy that fits your use-case and safety needs.

I like to hardcode development values in the tinkering phase and *change keys afterwards*. You never know what you leaked.

When my code's ready, I put configuration values in .env files and secrets in Secrets Manager.

Next chapter we look at authentication.

Serverless
authentication

You've got a feature that only a few people should use. How do you keep it safe?

Authentication.

It's easy in theory: Save an identifier on the client, send with every request, check against a stored value on the server.

In practice, authentication is hard.

Where do you save the identifier? How does the client get it? What authentication scheme do you use? What goes on the server? How do you keep it secure? What if you need to run authenticated code without the user?

Authentication is a deep rabbit hole. In this chapter, we look at the core ideas and build 2 examples.

What is authentication

A typical authentication system deals with everything from user identity, to access control, authorization, and keeping your system secure.

It's a big job :)

Identity answers the *"Who are you?"* question. The most important aspect of authentication systems. Can be as simple as an honor-based input field.

Access control answers the *"Can you access this system?"* question. You ask for proof of identity (like a password) and unlock restricted parts of your app.

Authorization answers the *"Which parts of the system can you use?"* question. Two schemes are common: role-based and scope-based authorization. They specify which users can do what.

Security underlies your authentication system. Without security, you've got nothing.

Typical concerns include leaking authentication tokens, interception attacks, impersonating users, revoking access, how your data behaves, and whether you can identify a breach.

Factors of authentication

Proof of identity is key to good authentication.

something the user *knows*, something the user *has*, something the user *is*

Each authentication factor[169] covers a different overlapping proof of identity. 2 factors is considered safe, 3 is best. Typical is 1 🏚

169 https://en.wikipedia.org/wiki/Authentication#Authentication_factors

Knowledge factors include hidden pass phrases like passwords, PINs, and security questions. You know the answer and verify the user knows too.

Ownership factors include ID cards, token apps on your phone, physical tokens, and email inboxes. You ask the user to prove they have something only they should have.

Inference factors include biometric identifiers like fingerprints, DNA, hand-written signatures, and other markers that uniquely identify a person.

Credit card + PIN is 2-factor authentication. You own the card and know the PIN.

Username + password is 1-factor. You know the username and know the password.

Passwordless email/sms login is 2-factor. You know the username and own the email inbox. Proof by unique link or pin.

Role-based and scope-based authorization

The 2nd job after access control is authorization. What can *this* user do?

Two flavors of authorization are common:

- **role-based** authorization depends on user types. Admins vs. paid users vs. freeloaders.
- **scope-based** authorization depends on fine-grained user properties. Enable subscriber dashboard or don't.

Technically they're the same – a user property. It's like utility vs. semantic classes in CSS. Debate until you're blue in the face, then pick what feels right :)

Role-based authorization is perfect for small projects. You need admins and everyone else. Being an admin comes with inherent rights.

Scope-based authorization is perfect for large projects with granular needs. Yes you're an admin, but admin of what?

In practice you'll see that roles get clunky and scopes are tedious. Like my dayjob gave me permission to configure CloudFront, but not to see what I'm doing. 😒

At an organizational level you end up with roles that act as bags of scopes. Engineers get scopes x, y, z, admins can do so and so, and users get user things.

Build your own auth

Let's build a basic serverless auth designed to be used as an API. It's the best way to get a feel for what it takes.

I'll share and explain the important code. You can see the full example on GitHub[170]. Use this CodeSandbox app[171] to try it out or go to serverlesshandbook.dev/claim to access interactive features.

You can test your implementation too. Change the Lambda base URL 😄

The auth flow

Traditional auth and API auth use a different medium to exchange tokens. Traditional auth uses cookies, API auth relies on JSON Web Tokens (JWT)[172] and Authorization headers.

The API approach works great with modern JavaScript apps, mobile clients, and other servers.

1. User sends username and password
2. Server checks against database
3. Returns fresh JWT token
4. Client adds token to every future request
5. Server checks token is valid before responding

This flow is secure because of the HTTPS encryption used at the protocol level. Without it, attackers could steal passwords and tokens by sniffing API requests.

170   https://github.com/Swizec/serverlesshandbook.dev/tree/master/
examples/serverless-auth-example
171 https://codesandbox.io/s/serverless-auth-example-9ipfb
172 https://jwt.io/

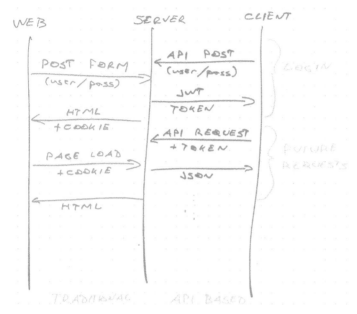

Figure 0.12: Authentication flow

Always use HTTPS and remember: *A JWT token on its own lets you impersonate a user.*

A note on password safety

You need to know the user's password to verify the user got it right. But *never* store a plain password.

A typical approach is to use a one-way hash[173] . Feed password into a cryptographic function, get unique value that's impossible to reverse.

173 https://en.wikipedia.org/wiki/Cryptographic_hash_function

Since the invention of rainbow tables[174] even one-way hashing is no longer secure. You can fight that with a salt.

```
// src/util.ts

// Hashing your password before saving is critical
// Hashing is one-way meaning you can never guess the
 ↪  password
// Adding a salt and the username guards against common
 ↪  passwords
export function hashPassword(username: string, password:
 ↪  string) {
  return sha256(
    `${password}${process.env.SALT}${username}\
    ${password}`
  ).toString()
}
```

Without a salt, the string password turns into the same hash for every app. Precomputed rainbow tables work like magic.

With a salt, the string password hashes uniquely to *your* app. Attackers need new rainbow tables, *if they can find the salt.*

Add the username and each hash is unique to your app *and* the user. Creating new rainbow tables for every user is not worth it.

174 https://en.wikipedia.org/wiki/Rainbow_table

That's when guessing becomes the easier approach. You can fight guessing with limits and timeouts on your login API.

Environment variables

We need 2 variables to build an auth system:

- a unique SALT for password hashing
- a unique JWT_SECRET for signing JWT tokens

We define them in `serverless.yml` to keep things simple. Use proper secrets handling[175] for production.

```
# serverless.yml
service: serverless-auth-example

provider:
  # ...
  environment:
    SALT: someRandomSecretString_useProperSecrets:)
    JWT_SECRET: useRealSecretsManagementPlease
```

175 /handling-secrets

Never share these with anyone. JWT_SECRET is all an attacker needs to impersonate a user.

auth.login **function**

Users need to be able to login – send an API request with their username and password to get a JWT token. We'll keep it similar to the REST API chapter[176].

```
# serverless.yml

functions:
  login:
    handler: dist/auth.login
    events:
      - http:
          path: login
          method: POST
          cors: true
```

We create a Lambda function called login that accepts POST requests and lives in the auth file.

176 /serverless-rest-api

```ts
// dist/auth.ts

// Logs you in based on username/password combo
// Creates user on first login
export const login = async (event: APIGatewayEvent) => {
  const { username, password } = \
      JSON.parse(event.body || "{}")

  // respond with error if username/password undefined

  // find user in database
  let user = await findUser(username)

  if (!user) {
    // user was not found, create
    user = await createUser(username, password)
  } else {
    // check credentials
    if (hashPassword(username, password) !== \
        user.password) {
      // <span class='emoji'
      ↪  data-emoji='rotating_light'> </span>
      return response(401, {
        status: "error",
        error: "Bad username/password combination",
      })
    }
  }

  // user was created or has valid credentials
```

```
  const token = jwt.sign(omit(user, "password"),
↪   process.env.JWT_SECRET!)

  return response(200, {
    user: omit(user, "password"),
    token,
  })
}
```

We grab username and password from request body and look for the user. findUser runs a database query, in our case a DynamoDB getItem.

If the user wasn't found, we create one and make sure to hashPassword() before saving.

If the user was found, we verify credentials by hashing the password and comparing with the stored value. We know passwords match when the hashPassword() method creates the same hash.

> This means you can never change your hashPassword() method unless you force users to reset their password.

Then we sign a JWT token with our secret and send it back. Make sure you don't send sensitive data like passwords to the client. Even hashed.

```
    // user was created or has valid credentials
  const token = jwt.sign(omit(user, "password"),
↪   process.env.JWT_SECRET!)

  return response(200, {
    user: omit(user, "password"),
    token,
  })
```

We're using the jsonwebtoken[177] library to create the token.

You can try it in the CodeSandbox[178] . Pick a username, add a password, see it work. Then try with a different password.

auth.verify **function**

For authentication to work across page reloads, you have to store the JWT token. These can expire or get revoked by the server.

Clients use the verify API to validate a session every time they initialize. A page reload on the web.

When you know the session is valid, you treat the user as logged in. Ask for a username/password otherwise.

177 https://github.com/auth0/node-jsonwebtoken
178 https://codesandbox.io/s/serverless-auth-example-9ipfb

serverless.yml definition is almost the same:

```
# serverless.yml

functions:
    # ...
  verify:
    handler: dist/auth.verify
    events:
      - http:
          path: verify
          method: POST
          cors: true
```

Function called verify that accepts POST requests and lives in auth.ts.

```
// src/auth.ts

// Verifies you have a valid JWT token
export const verify = async (event: APIGatewayEvent) \
    => {
  const { token } = JSON.parse(event.body || "{}")
```

```
// respond with error if token undefined

try {
  jwt.verify(token, process.env.JWT_SECRET!)
  return response(200, { status: "valid" })
} catch (err) {
  return response(401, err)
}
}
```

Verifying a JWT token with jsonwebtoken[179] throws an error for bad tokens. Anything from a bad secret, to tampering, and token expiration.

private.hello function

This is where it gets fun – verifying authentication for private APIs.

We make an API that says hello to the user.

```
# serverless.yml
```

179 https://github.com/auth0/node-jsonwebtoken

```
functions:
  privateHello:
    handler: dist/private.hello
    events:
      - http:
          path: private
          method: GET
          cors: true
```

Function accepts GET requests and lives in the `private.ts` file. It looks like this:

```
// src/private.ts

export async function hello(event: APIGatewayEvent) {
  // returns JWT token payload
  const user = checkAuth(event) as User

  if (user) {
    return response(200, {
      message: `Hello ${user.username}`,
    })
  } else {
    return response(401, {
      status: "error",
      error: "This is a private resource",
```

```
        })
    }
}
```

The checkAuth method takes our request, verifies its JWT token, and returns the payload. A user in our case.

If user is authorized, we say hello, otherwise return an error.

checkAuth is where we read a token from the Authorization header and verify it looks good.

```
// src/util.ts

// Used to verify a request is authenticated
export function checkAuth(event: APIGatewayEvent):\
    boolean | User {
  const bearer = event.headers["Authorization"]

  if (bearer) {
    try {
      const decoded = jwt.verify(
        // Bearer prefix from Authorization header
        bearer.replace(/^Bearer /, ""),
        process.env.JWT_SECRET!
      )
```

```
      // We saved user info in the token
    return decoded as User
  } catch (err) {
    return false
  }
  } else {
    return false
  }
}
```

The Authorization header holds our token – Authorization: Bearer <token>. If the header is empty, return false.

The jwt.verify() method verifies the token was valid. Checks that it was created with our secret, wasn't tampered with, and hasn't expired.

verify decodes the token for us, which means we can see the user's username without a database query. 🤷

Use an auth provider

An auth provider like Auth0, Okta, AWS Cognito, Firebase Auth, and others makes your integration more complex. But *you* don't have to worry about password security and user management.

And if a big provider gets hacked, your app is one among thousands. Feels less bad eh? 😇

The key difference with a provider is the 3-way trust model. Users authenticate with a provider and send you a JWT token.

But you're not the authority.

That means a login dance between your server and the auth provider. You'll need to send your own JWT token to ask if the user's token is valid.

Exact integration depends on your provider of choice. I recommend following their documentation.

If performance is critical, this option is not great. You're adding API requests to every private call.

An example integration

Here's what I do to create users on Auth0 when you purchase a course on Gumroad, a payments provider. It's the provider <> lambda part of the flow.

The course platform runs in the browser, which means the user <> lambda connection wasn't necessary. A benefit of using a provider 😊

Gumroad sends a POST request to AWS Lambda on every purchase. It runs this function:

```
export const pingHandler = async (
    event: APIGatewayEvent
): Promise<APIResponse> => {
    const ping: GumroadPing = qs.parse(event.body!);

    if (ping.product_permalink in PRODUCTS) {
        // create user from Gumroad data
        const user = await upsertUser(ping);

        if (user) {
            // initialize Auth0 server client
            const auth0 = await getAuth0Client();
            const roleId =
↪   PRODUCTS[ping.product_permalink];
```

```
            // give access to the course
          await auth0.assignRolestoUser(
              { id: user.user_id! },
              {
                  roles: [roleId],
              }
          );
      }
  }

    return response(200, {});
};
```

The function parses data from Gumroad, creates a user on Auth0, and assigns the right role. I treat roles as scopes ← which courses can this user access?

Auth0 Client

Getting the Auth0 client means authenticating the server through a shared secret. Like a username and password.

```
async function getAuth0Client() {
    const secrets = await auth0Tokens();
```

```
const auth0 = new ManagementClient({
    domain: `${secrets.domain}.auth0.com`,
    clientId: secrets.clientId,
    clientSecret: secrets.clientSecret,
    scope: "read:users update:users create:users",
});

return auth0;
}
```

getAuth0Tokens talks to AWS Secrets Manager to retrieve se-crets. We feed those to a new ManagementClient, which will use them to sign JWT tokens for future requests.

Auth0 will be able to jwt.verify() to see that we know the right secrets.

A ManagementClient can manages users. For authentication you'd use the AuthenticationClient.

We ask for as little permission as possible. If someone steals these secrets, or the code, they can't do much.

If an attacker tries to expand permissions, Auth0 config says *"hey this client can't do that even if it asks"*

Create user

Creating a user is a matter of calling the right methods. Look for user, create if not found.

```
async function upsertUser(purchaseData: GumroadPing) {
    const auth0 = await getAuth0Client();

    // find user
    const users = await
↪   auth0.getUsersByEmail(purchaseData.email);

    // create if not found
    if (users.length > 0) {
        return users[0];
    } else {
        return auth0.createUser({
            // user data
        });
    }
}
```

What approach to choose?

Hard to say.

Building your own is fun the first 2 or 3 times. User management and authorization is where you go ouch and think *"I have better shit to do damn it"*.

Libraries help :)

An auth provider has more engineers to think about these problems and give you a nice experience. But integration is more complex.

Whatever you do, don't build your own cryptography. ✌

Appendix: Databases in more detail

Read additional details and insights that didn't fit into the main chapter on databases.

Flat file database

The simplest way to store data is a flat file database[180]. Even if you call it "just organized files".

Serverless systems don't have drives to store files so these flat file databases aren't a popular choice. You'd have to use S3 or similar, which negates some of the built-in advantages.

We mention them here because they're often a great choice and most engineers forget they exist.

180 https://en.wikipedia.org/wiki/Flat-file_database

Advantages of flat files

Compared to other databases, flat files have zero overhead. Your data goes straight to storage without your database adding any logic on top.

This gives flat files amazing write performance. As long as you're adding data to the end of a file.

Optimizing file access for speed comes down to your operating system. Performance mostly has to do with memory paging[181] , filesystem[182] configuration, direct memory access[183] , and hardware-level optimizations.

The end result is:

- **fast append performance**, because you stream data from memory to drive without processor involvement
- **fast read performance for common reads**, because computers use their memory as read-through cache. Once you read a file, subsequent reads come from much faster memory
- **fast search for predicted lookups**, because you can structure your files in a way that makes common lookups instant
- **great scalability**, because you can spread your data over as many servers as you'd like

181 https://en.wikipedia.org/wiki/Paging
182 https://en.wikipedia.org/wiki/File_system
183 https://en.wikipedia.org/wiki/Direct_memory_access

Disadvantages of flat files

Where flat files struggle are data updates.

To add a line at the beginning of a file, you have to move the whole thing. To change a line in the middle, you have to update everything that comes after.

Another problem is lack of a query interface.

You have to read all your files to compare, analyze, and search. If you didn't think of a use-case beforehand, you're left with a slow search through everything.

- **slow data updates**, because you often have to rewrite more than just the changes
- **no data shape guarantees**, because you can store individual data items any way you like. If you change your schema, you have to deal with inconsistencies, or rewrite your data
- **slow broad reads**, because you lose benefits of read-through-cache, if you read data across your entire database with random patterns
- **no ACID compliance** unless you build it yourself at the application layer

How to use flat files

A flat-file database happens any time you write data to files in a structured manner. Photos on your phone are a great example.

When you take a photo, your phone stores it as a file. Filenames often follow a naming convention – IMG_0001, IMG_0002, etc. Some cameras add dates.

Now you can sequentially access photos. Start at the beginning, go until the end. You can even keep track of how far you've gotten so you can jump ahead next time.

What about finding all photos from a certain date?

That's why images contain EXIF metadata[184] – information about date, time, GPS location, even phone orientation. It's all stored in the file in a structured way.

To find images from a certain date, you can search through your files and look at the metadata they contain.

Hierarchical and flat file organization

You can speed up seek operations by adding common search keys to your file names.

A good example is organizing photos by year - month - date. Each year is a directory containing directories for months. Each of those contains directories for days. Those contain photos.

Hierarchical storage slashes search speed by a huge factor. You can jump right into a specific category (date).

184 https://en.wikipedia.org/wiki/Exif

But hierarchical storage makes scanning harder. Counting all images now requires a recursive search through directories.

A better approach might be encoding your meta data in the filename. Something like `IMG_${year}-${month}-${day}-001.jpg`.

Gives you quick access to specific dates *and* fast scans across many.

When you should store data in flat files

Due to its low overhead, flat file storage is a great choice when you're looking for speed and simplicity.

Use flat files when:

1. You need fast append-only writes
2. You have simple querying requirements
3. You read data more often than you write data
4. You write data that you rarely read

Avoid flat files when:

1. You need to cross-reference data or use complex queries
2. You need fast access across your entire database
3. Your data often changes

No. 3 is the flat file database killer.

The most common use cases for flat files are logs, large datasets, and large binary files (image, video, etc).

You often append logs and rarely read them. You store large datasets as structured files for easy sharing. You save images and rarely update, and they contain orders of magnitude more binary data than structured metadata.

Relational databases – RDBMS

Relational databases[185] are the most common type of database people think of when you say "database". Data lives in a structured data model and many features exist to optimize performance.

185 https://en.wikipedia.org/wiki/Relational_database

Choosing a relational database for your business data is almost always the right decision.

Advantages of relational databases

Relational databases have been around since the 1970's. They're battle tested, reliable, and can adapt to almost any workload.

Some modern solutions incorporate features from the NoSQL universe to become even more versatile. Postgres[186] is a great example since it often outperforms NoSQL solutions on performance benchmarks.

The defining feature of relational databases is their relational data model. The relational data model makes it easy to model complex data using small isolated concepts. Everything else stems from there.

Decades of research have gone into optimizing relational database performance. Down to features like reserving empty space on a hard drive so data commonly used together sits together to make access faster 🤓

With a relational database, you get:

- **fast write performance**, because most systems write to memory first and save to drive later

186 https://en.wikipedia.org/wiki/PostgreSQL

- **fast read performance**, because you can build lookup data structures (indexes)[187] for common queries
- **flexible querying**, because you can use a query language (usually SQL) to access any data in any configuration
- **strict ACID compliance**, because it's a core design objective
- some **logical data validation**, because you can describe the shape of your data and have the database enforce its consistency

Disadvantages of relational databases

Benefits of relational databases come with the downside of being harder to use, requiring more expertise to tune performance, and some loss in flexibility.

You can create a database that's fast as lightning, or shoot yourself in the foot.

Main disadvantages are:

- **high level of complexity**, because it's easy to get started and the fine-tuning rabbit hole goes forever deep
- **performance traps at scale**, because a database that's blazing fast at 10,000 entries, might crawl to a halt at 10,000,000 entries

187 https://en.wikipedia.org/wiki/Database_index

- **tradeoffs between read and write performance**, because you can get more read performance by sacrificing write performance and vice-versa. Mostly to do with index building
- **data shape inflexibility**, because with a typical configuration, you have to redefine the shape of your data every time you add a property
- **lack of horizontal scalability**, because relational databases can't give you most of their benefits when split across many servers

A common solution for flexibility is to add a blobby JSON field to every model. You lose automatic data integrity and performance optimization on that field, but gain the flexibility to store any data in any shape. Perfect use-case for less important metadata.

How to use a relational DB

We'll focus on the basics here. You should approach the rest with just-in-time learning – run into a problem, learn how to solve it. ✌

You start with a database server.

A database server

Since you don't want to run your own servers (the whole point of serverless), you'll need a provider. 3rd party services are okay, if your serverless provider doesn't offer their own.

Using a "native" service cuts down on network overhead and makes your system faster. With some luck, your provider runs the database and cloud functions in the same datacenter. Perhaps even on the same physical machine.

In the AWS world, I've found RDS – Relational Database Service[188] works great. Gives you a stable provisioned database server.

Despite giving you a reserved database instance, RDS still offers advantages over rolling your own:

- drive space grows as necessary
- regular updates run automatically
- if a server falls over, RDS brings up a new one with the same data
- automatic backups
- easy restore from backup
- optional multi-zone replication for extra reliability (copies your DB over several data centers)

A more serverless version of RDS is Amazon Aurora DB[189]. Implemented as a layer on top of RDS, it scales your database based on usage. Even shutting down when nothing's happening. Less expensive for intermittent workloads *and* you don't have to predict how much power you'll need.

188 https://aws.amazon.com/rds/
189 https://aws.amazon.com/rds/aurora/

When choosing which relational database software to use, **always choose Postgres**. It's open source, crazy fast, and with great support for modern NoSQL features.

https://twitter.com/Swizec/status/1210371195889049600

Model your data

The next step is to model your data.

How to model your data is as much an art as it is a science. Sort of a mix between domain modeling[190] and object modeling[191] .

Models also known as tables store each property as a column. Model instances live as rows inside those tables.

Let's say you're building a blog. You have authors and posts.

Each author has an id (automatically assigned), a created_at timestamp, and a name. Each post also has an id (automatically assigned), a created_at timestamp, a title, and some content.

Ids are numbers, timestamps are timestamps, the rest is text. A relational database ensures that's always true so you can expect valid data.

190 https://en.wikipedia.org/wiki/Domain_model
191 https://en.wikipedia.org/wiki/Object_model

To create a connection between models, you use a foreign key[192] .
A column that points to the identifier of a different table.

For authors and posts you get a schema like this:

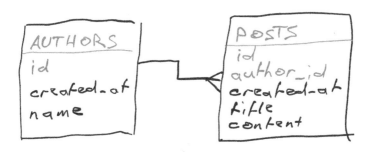

Which in SQL – Standard Query Language[193] – looks something
like this:

```
CREATE TABLE IF NOT EXISTS "authors" (
    "id" serial,
    "created_at" timestamp,
    "name" text,
    PRIMARY KEY( id )
);
```

192 https://en.wikipedia.org/wiki/Foreign_key
193 https://en.wikipedia.org/wiki/SQL

```
CREATE TABLE IF NOT EXISTS "posts" (
    "id" serial,
    "created_at" timestamp,
    "title" text,
    "content" text,
    "author_id" integer,
    PRIMARY KEY( id, author_id ),
    FOREIGN KEY ( author_id ) REFERENCES authors( id )
);
```

That creates 2 empty tables in your database and connects them via a foreign key. Postgres automatically increments identifiers and ensures uniqueness as you insert new rows.

Having the posts table "belong to" (point at) the authors table means each author can have multiple posts.

Query your data

You interact with a relational database primarily through SQL[194]. Many web server frameworks come with an ORM[195] – object-relational-mapping – layer on top of SQL that simplifies common operations.

Regardless of using an ORM, you'll have to know SQL for anything complex. At least have an understanding of how it works.

194 https://en.wikipedia.org/wiki/SQL
195 https://en.wikipedia.org/wiki/Object-relational_mapping

A basic query that fetches all `authors` looks like this:

```
SELECT * FROM authors;
```

Writing keywords in all caps is customary but not required. I think it stems from ye olden times before syntax highlighting.

To fetch just names, you'd do this:

```
SELECT name FROM authors;
```

Select *what* from *where*. SQL is meant to be readable as natural English. Used to be the main user interface after all.

To fetch authors created after a certain date, something like this:

```
SELECT name FROM authors WHERE created_at\
>= '2019-12-26';
```

You can put almost any condition in a WHERE clause.

Where life gets real tricky real fast is selecting data from multiple tables. You have to use SQL joins[196] , which are based on set arithmetic.

If you want a list of post titles and dates with each author:

```
SELECT a.name, p.title, p.created_at
FROM authors a, posts po
WHERE p.author_id = a.id;
```

This is called an inner join[197] where you take a cartesian join combining every row in authors with every row in posts and filter away the non-matches.

Those are some basics that cover most use-cases. It takes some practice to use SQL effectively so practice away :)

196 https://en.wikipedia.org/wiki/Join_(SQL)
197 https://en.wikipedia.org/wiki/Join_(SQL)#Inner_join

Speed up your data

Relational databases use a query planner[198] to execute SQL queries as efficiently as possible. You often don't even have to think about performance.

Common ways to speed up your database include:

1. **Adding indexes** – data structures that help your database find data matching specific queries. Depending on the type of index you choose, it can behave like a directory tree, or like a hash table
2. **Denormalization** – storing properties often used together in the same table even if it means duplicating some data. Like having an author name field in each post.
3. **Partitioning** – telling your database how to chunk a large table into files so common lookups read from the same physical file

Tuning a relational database for performance is a whole field of software engineering so I wouldn't worry about it too much. Learn about it when you need to ✌

When you should store data in a relational DB

Choosing a relational database is almost always the correct choice.

198 https://en.wikipedia.org/wiki/Query_plan

Use relational DBs when:

1. You don't know how you're using your data
2. You benefit from data integrity
3. You need good performance up to hundreds of million entries
4. Your app fits in a single data center (availability zone)
5. You often use different objects together

Avoid relational DBs when:

1. You're storing lots of binary data (images, video)
2. You don't care about data integrity
3. You don't want to invest in initial setup
4. You just need a quick way to save some data
5. You have so much data it doesn't fit on 1 server

This makes relational databases the perfect choice for most applications. You wouldn't use them to store files, but should consider it for metadata about those files. They're also not a great choice for fast append-only writes like logs or tweets.

I wouldn't worry about number 5. If you ever reach the scale where your data doesn't fit in a single database, you'll have a team to solve the problem for you :)

The NoSQL approach

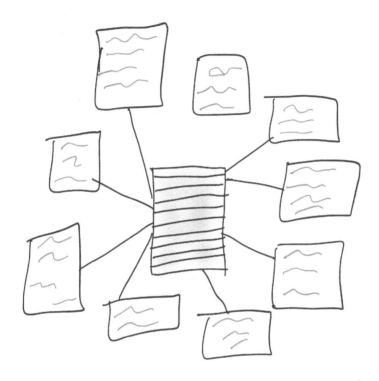

"NoSQL" is a broad range of technologies built for different purposes with different design goals in mind. A sort of catch-all for any database that doesn't use relational data models.

Yes even flat file storage is a sort of NoSQL database.

Wikipedia offers a great description of NoSQL databases[199]

199 https://en.wikipedia.org/wiki/NoSQL

The data structures used by NoSQL databases are different from those used by default in relational databases, making some operations faster in NoSQL. The particular suitability of a given NoSQL database depends on the problem it must solve.

This variety is where NoSQL differs most from relational databases. Where relational databases aim to fit most use cases, NoSQL often aims to solve a specific problem.

Flavors of NoSQL

You can classify NoSQL databases in 4 broad categories:

1. **key:value store** that works like a dictionary. A unique key points to a stored value. Offers fast read/write performance and is often used as a caching layer in front of a relational database. Some solutions offer sortable keys so you can perform data scans.
2. **document store** that maps unique keys to documents. Basically key:value stores that allow complex values. They often support a query language that lets you search based on value contents, not just the key.
3. **graph database** that stores graph data structures efficiently. Useful for data models with a lot of circular references like social graphs or road maps.

4. **wide column database** that is a sort of mix between a document store and a relational database. Keys map to objects that all fit a schema, but that schema isn't prescriptive. There's no guarantee every object has every column, but you always know every column that might exist.

Everything else is a variation on these themes. Most modern databases support multiple models.

You can stringify JSON objects into a key:value store to create a document store without querying support. Or you can store simple values in a document DB to create a key:value store with too much overhead.

There's nothing stopping you from forcing a graph to live inside a table database either. 😅

Which NoSQL flavor should you pick?

It really depends. What are you trying to do?

I would prioritize a hosted fully managed database solution that my serverless provider offers. This cuts down on networking overhead, just like the RDBMS section, and makes your life easier because there's one less thing to manage.

Then I would pick whatever fits my use case.

Use key:value stores when you need blazing fast data with low overhead. Great for implementing caching layers and queue systems. Redis[200] is a great choice here. Memcached[201] , if you just need cache.

I often use Redis *and* Memcached in real world projects.

Use a document DB or wide column store when you want a generic database for business data that isn't a relational database. You get the benefit of flexibility and horizontal scalability. No schemas to prepare in advance and little thought about optimizing queries.

You pay for that 3 years down the line with inconsistent data. Learned my lesson ✌️

MongoDB[202] is a good document/object store. Amazon DynamoDB[203] and Google's Bigtable[204] are great examples of wide column stores.

Use a graph DB when you're *actually* storing graph data. While you can fit a graph into any database (I've tried), you're going to benefit from graph querying support that comes with a real graph DB. They're optimized for just that use-case.

Haven't had a good excuse to use one yet, but I've heard Neo4j[205] is great.

200 https://en.wikipedia.org/wiki/Redis
201 https://en.wikipedia.org/wiki/Memcached
202 https://en.wikipedia.org/wiki/MongoDB
203 https://en.wikipedia.org/wiki/Amazon_DynamoDB
204 https://en.wikipedia.org/wiki/Bigtable
205 https://en.wikipedia.org/wiki/Neo4j

My favorite advantage of most NoSQL databases is their wonderful integration with the JavaScript/TypeScript ecosystem. Most let you store JSON blobs, which means there's no translation between JavaScript objects and database objects.

That makes your life much easier compared to a SQL-based solution.

Disadvantages of NoSQL databases

Disadvantages of NoSQL mostly come from its advantages. Funny how that works.

The simplicity of key:value stores gives you speed at the cost of not being able to store complex data.

The write speed of document databases comes at the cost of some ACID compliance. Often using the eventual consistency[206] model to write fast and propagate to other instances and objects later.

The ease of schema-less development comes at the cost of inconsistent data. If you want entries to look the same, you often have to take care of it yourself.

NoSQL databases also struggle with relational data. And it turns out most real world data is relational.

206 https://en.wikipedia.org/wiki/Eventual_consistency

You *can* store relational data in a NoSQL database, but it can be cumbersome to query. Often there's no support for joins so you have to search through different parts of your database and assemble objects by hand.

How to use a NoSQL DB

How to use a NoSQL DB depends on which database you pick. I recommend using an official library.

Serverless Handbook focuses on the AWS ecosystem with the serverless framework, so we're going to look at DynamoDB.

DynamoDB is a great choice for saving JSON data, scales well, works fast, and is pretty cheap to use. And unlike RDS, you can set it up using `serverless.yml`.

Create a DynamoDB table

To define a new DynamoDB table, add this to your config.

```
provider:
    environment:
```

```
      DATA_TABLE:
↪   ${self:service}-data-${self:provider.stage}
    iamRoleStatements:
      - Effect: Allow
        Action:
          - dynamodb:Query
          - dynamodb:Scan
          - dynamodb:GetItem
          - dynamodb:PutItem
          - dynamodb:UpdateItem
          - dynamodb:DeleteItem
        Resource: "arn:aws:dynamodb:${opt:region,
↪   self:provider.region}:*:table/\

↪   ${self:provider.environment.DATA_TABLE}"
```

Using environment variables for table names makes them easier to use. Postfixing with the stage lets you replicate configuration between development and production without messing up your data.

iamRoleStatements give your app permission to use this table.

You then need to create the actual table:

```
resources:
    Resources:
        DataTable:
            Type: "AWS::DynamoDB::Table"
            Properties:
                AttributeDefinitions:
                    - AttributeName: dataId
                      AttributeType: S
                KeySchema:
                    - AttributeName: dataId
                      KeyType: HASH
                ProvisionedThroughput:
                    ReadCapacityUnits: 1
                    WriteCapacityUnits: 1
                TableName:
↪   ${self;provider.environment.DATA_TABLE}
```

You're defining an AWS resource of type DynamoDB::Table with a
required dataId column that's going to be used as a key. HASH keys
give you key:value lookups, RANGE keys are easier to scan through.

Each table can have 2 keys at most.

Name your table using the environment variable defined earlier
for consistency. ✌️

Save some data

Saving data to a DynamoDB table can be a little cumbersome with Amazon's default SDK. There doesn't seem to be a clear best library so I've been writing small wrappers myself.

You save data using upserts: If a key exists, the data is updated. If it doesn't, it's created. I recommend using uuid[207] for identifiers.

Something like this:

```
export const createData = async (_: any, params:
↪  CreateDataParams) => {
    const dataId = uuidv4();

    const result = await updateItem({
        TableName: process.env.DATE_TABLE!,
        Key: {
            dataId
        },
        UpdateExpression: "SET dataName = :dataName,
↪  createdAt = :createdAt",
        ExpressionAttributeValues: {
            ":dataName": params.dataName,
            ":createdAt": new Date().toISOString()
        },
        ReturnValues: "ALL_NEW"
```

207 https://en.wikipedia.org/wiki/Universally_unique_identifier

```
    });

    return result.Attributes;
};
```

Create an identifier with the uuid library, run an update expression on the appropriate table. Return the entire new row.

UpdateExpression and ExpressionAttributeValues is split into two objects to help DynamoDB prevent injection attacks. Also helps with performance.

updateItem is a wrapper I built around the official SDK. You can see the code on GitHub[208] . I'll turn it into a library once I'm happy with the ergonomics.

You now have data saved in the database.

To update this data you have to create a similar method that gets your dataId as a parameter and uses it to run an updateItem query. Make sure you aren't always creating a new identifier.

---

208   https://github.com/Swizec/markdownlandingpage.com/blob/master/
server/src/dynamodb.ts#L35

Read some data

Unlike with a relational database, you have a choice of *scanning*
and *getting*. A scan lets you search for entries that match a criteria.
Getting lets you fetch an exact entry.

Something like this:

```
export const allDataWithName = async ({ dataName }) => {
    const result = await scanItems({
        TableName: process.env.DATA_TABLE!,
        FilterExpression: "#dataName = :dataName",
        ExpressionAttributeNames: {
            "#dataName": "dataName"
        },
        ExpressionAttributeValues: {
            ":dataName": dataName
        }
    });

    return result.Items;
};
```

scanItems is again a little helper method I wrote[209] . It needs to
do more because this is quite cumbersome.

209   https://github.com/Swizec/markdownlandingpage.com/blob/master/
server/src/dynamodb.ts#L73

But it lets you *scan* through a table looking for entries that fit a criteria.

You can use the `getItem` approach when you know exactly what you're looking for.

```
export const data = async ({ dataId }) => {
    const result = await getItem({ Key: { dataId } });

    if (!result.Item) {
        return {};
    }

    return result.Item
};
```

Notice how we get a JavaScript object that we can return without modification. That's the beauty of NoSQL. ✌

Blockchain

Blockchain is the new kid on the block. Usually mixed up with cryptocurrencies and financial speculation, it's actually a solid way to share and store data.

You've probably used one before ☞ git.

That's right, git[210] and The Blockchain[211] share the same underlying data structure: a merkle tree.

A merkle tree[212] stores data in a cryptographically verified sequence of blocks. Each new block contains a cryptographic hash of the previous block.

That means you can always verify your data. Follow the chain and validate every hash. Once you reach the initial block, you know your chain is valid.

As a result you don't need a central authority to tell you the current state of your data. Clients can independently decide, if the data

210 https://en.wikipedia.org/wiki/Git
211 https://en.wikipedia.org/wiki/Blockchain
212 https://en.wikipedia.org/wiki/Merkle_tree

they have is valid. Often by assuming the longest valid chain is correct.

Adding a consensus algorithm makes the process even more robust. When you add new data, how many servers have to agree that the data is valid?

The result is a slow, but robustly decentralized database.

I wouldn't use the blockchain to store real data just yet, but it's an exciting space to watch. Blockstack[213] is a great way to get started.

---

213 https://blockstack.org/

Glossary

The Serverless Handbook uses lots of terms that might be unfamiliar. I introduce them at first use and understand new words are hard.

Refer here any time you encounter an unfamiliar word. If something's missing ping me on twitter @swizec.

Words and phrases in alphabetical order.

- **ACID** short for atomicity-consistency-isolation-durability, a model of database correctness
- **API** short for Application Programming Interface, use to mean everything from the URL structure of a server to the public interface of a class or function
- **API Gateway** the AWS service that routes HTTP requests from public URLs to internal services
- **ARN** short for Amazon Resource Name, the globally unique identifier for AWS items
- **AWS** amazon web services
- **CDN** short for Content Distribution Network, an approach to serving static files that improves latency
- **CLI** short for Command Line Interface, the terminal you type commands into

- **CORS** a security protocol that limits which domains can access certain assets
- **CPU** short for central processing unit, the part of computers that does most of the work
- **CRUD** short for Create Read Update Delete, a typical set of operations apps need to support
- **CloudWatch** the AWS service that collects and displays basic logs and metrics from every other service
- **DB** short for database
- **DLQ** short for Dead Letter Queue, a special queue used to hold bad messages for further debugging
- **DNS** short for Domain Name System/Server, it translates domains to IP addresses
- **DX** short for developer experience, a catch-all for how it feels to work with a technology
- **Go** a popular lightweight language for server programming
- **I/O** short for input/output, the process of reading and writing to an external medium like a hard drive or database
- **IP address** the globally unique identifier for a computer on the internet
- **JSON** a popular data format based on JavaScript objects
- **JVM** short for Java Virtual Machine, the runtime environment for Java applications
- **QA** short for Quality Assurance, used to mean both the process and the teams doing it
- **RDS** short for Relational Database Service, an AWS service for hosting relational databases like Postgres and MySQL
- **S3** the AWS static file hosting service
- **SNS** short for Simple Notification Service, a messaging pub/sub service on AWS

- **SQS** short for Simple Queue Service, a messaging queue service on AWS
- **SSL** the encrypted communication layer used on the web
- **UI** short for user interface
- **VPS** short for Virtual Private Server, a type of shared hosting
- **apache** a common web server popular with the open source community
- **azure** Microsoft's cloud and serverless computing platform
- **blockchain** a distributed ledger used for cryptocurrencies, data storage, and smart contracts
- **cache** a fast data storage service or app for temporary data used to improve performance
- **chrome puppeteer** a library used to automate browser tasks with Chrome
- **cloud function** another name for a unit in function-as-a-service serverless computing
- **cloudfront** AWS's CDN service
- **compute** a fuzzy term for unit of computation used to talk about pricing and performance
- **devops** is a set of practices that combines development and IT operations
- **docker** a popular computer virtualization software and toolkit
- **dynamodb** a wide-table NoSQL database service on AWS
- **edge workers** a type of cloud function that works like a CDN and aims to reduce latency
- **exponential backoff** a common approach to reducing load on a 3rd party service that is struggling
- **firebase** Google's suite of backend-as-a-service offerings

- **git** a common version control system
- **graphql** an API protocol based on queries commonly used to increase client power and flexibility
- **hashing function** a secure method of uniquely encoding a string in a way that cannot be reversed
- **heroku** a popular platform-as-a-service provider
- **http** short for HyperText Transfer Protocol, the underlying protocol of the web
- **https** the secure encrypted version of http that uses SSL
- **jamstack** Javascript And Markdown stack, a stack of technologies used for modern static-first websites
- **kubernetes** a popular toolkit for managing servers and containers
- **lambda function** a unit in function-as-a-service serverless computing, synonym for cloud function
- **netlify** a jamstack and serverless provider, popularized the jamstack approach
- **nginx** a popular web server created in 2004 to address Apache's performance issues
- **nosql** an umbrella term for databases that trade ACID compliance for specific performance or usability gains
- **PaaS/platform as a service** a type of hosting that aims to solve infrastructure complexity
- **poison pill** an unprocessable message or request
- **queue** a data structure that processes messages in order, also used as shorthand for a service or application that acts as a queue
- **rainbow tables** a pre-computed cache of hashes used to reverse hashed passwords
- **relational database** a popular approach to storing business

data since the 1970's, often synonymous with the concept of a database

- **rest** a common approach to designing web APIs
- **server** depending on context, a machine running software that serves internet requests, or the software itself
- **serverless** an on-demand hosting environment
- **ssh** short for secure shell, a protocol for remotely controlling services
- **upsert** an operation that inserts a new object or updates an existing object with the same identifier
- **vercel** a jamstack and serverless provider
- **yak shaving** a useless activity that indirectly helps you solve a larger problem

Lightning Source UK Ltd.
Milton Keynes UK
UKHW020342131121
393864UK00007B/250